GULLIVER'S TRAVELS

Brian Tippett

MACMILLAN

For Glenys, Mark, Clare and Paul

First published 1989

Published by
MACMILLAN EDUCATION LTD
Houndmills, Basingstoke, Hampshire RG21 2XS
and London
Companies and representatives
throughout the world

Printed in Hong Kong

British Library Cataloguing in Publication Data
Tippett, Brian
Gulliver's travels.—(The Critics debate).
1. Fiction in English. Swift, Jonathan.
Gulliver's travels – Critical studies
I. Title   II. Series
823'.5
ISBN 0–333–38444–X
ISBN 0–333–38445–8 Pbk

Contents

General Editor's Preface   7
A Note on Text and References   9
Introduction   11

Part One: Survey   18

    Author-centred Approaches   18
    Formal and Rhetorical Approaches   27
    Historical and Contextual Approaches   41

Part Two: Appraisal   61

    Introduction: The World Made Strange   61
    A Children's Classic?   67
    Worlds Past and Present   73
    Into the World of Words   82

References and Further Reading   92
Index   98

General Editor's Preface

OVER THE last few years the practice of literary criticism has become hotly debated. Methods developed earlier in the century and before have been attacked and the word 'crisis' has been drawn upon to describe the present condition of English Studies. That such a debate is taking place is a sign of the subject discipline's health. Some would hold that the situation necessitates a radical alternative approach which naturally implies a 'crisis situation'. Others would respond that to employ such terms is to precipitate or construct a false position. The debate continues but it is not the first. 'New Criticism' acquired its title because it attempted something fresh calling into question certain practices of the past. Yet the practices it attacked were not entirely lost or negated by the new critics. One factor becomes clear: English Studies is a pluralistic discipline.

What are students coming to advanced work in English for the first time to make of all this debate and controversy? They are in danger of being overwhelmed by the cross-currents of critical approaches as they take up their study of literature. The purpose of this series is to help delineate various critical approaches to specific literary texts. Its authors are from a variety of critical schools and have approached their task in a flexible manner. Their aim is to help the reader come to terms with the variety of criticism and to introduce him or her to further reading on the subject and to a fuller evaluation of a particular text by illustrating the way it has been approached in a number of contexts. In the first part of the book a critical survey is given of some of the major ways the text has been appraised. This is done sometimes in a thematic manner, sometimes according to various 'schools' or 'approaches'. In the second part the authors provide their own appraisals of the text from their stated critical standpoint, allowing the reader the knowledge of their own particular approaches from which

their views may in turn be evaluated. The series therein hopes
to introduce and to elucidate criticism of authors and texts being
studied and to encourage participation as the critics debate.

Michael Scott

A Note on Text and References

IT IS WORTH recalling that what is now universally known as *Gulliver's Travels* was originally published in 1726 as *Travels into Several Remote Nations of the World* by Lemuel Gulliver, without acknowledgement of Swift's authorship. The text used here is that of the Penguin edition by Peter Dixon and John Chalker with an Introduction by Michael Foot (Harmondsworth, 1967). For the convenience of readers using other editions, I have in some cases given references to voyage and chapter number as well as to the page number of the Penguin edition, thus: II.iv.159 or *GT* II.iv.159. In the final section of the Appraisal quotations are from the text given in volume XI of the standard edition of the *Prose Writings of Jonathan Swift* edited by Herbert Davis (14 volumes, Oxford, 1939–68), which preserves typographic features (e.g. initial capital letters for nouns and italics for names) of an eighteenth-century edition.

Works of criticism and other secondary sources are referred to in abbreviated style by author's surname and date of publication. This enables reference to be made to the bibliography at the end of the book. Where titles are referred to in more than one section, details are given in one place only in the bibliography.

Introduction

WHEN IT first appeared in 1726 *Gulliver's Travels* immediately seized public attention, prompting a flood of oral and written comment which has continued unabated until the present day. By the time, nine years later, when the prefatory Letter to Sympson (dated 1727) was added to a new edition, the volume of secondary literature surrounding the book had grown to such an extent that Gulliver could with justice complain:

> You are loading our carrier every week with Libels, and Keys, and Reflections and Memoirs, and Second Parts; wherein I see myself accused of reflecting upon great states-folk; of degrading human nature . . ., and of abusing the female sex; I find likewise, that the writers of those bundles are not agreed among themselves. (p.39)

What is described in this thumb-nail sketch of the contemporary critical debate was, in volume, direction and emphasis, a foretaste of what was to follow. A rough count of the entries under Swift's name in the *Cambridge Bibliography of English Literature* shows that up to 1969 well over 750 books and articles about him had been published, that of these over 200 appeared between 1900 and 1945 and more than twice as many in the twenty-four years after that. Critics have, if anything, been even more prolific in the years since 1969 and the score must now exceed a thousand books and essays, of which a large proportion inevitably have something to say about Swift's most celebrated book and perhaps the greatest English prose satire. This kind of record could no doubt be matched by other major works of literature, which is not altogether surprising for it reflects the development of English Studies as one of the most popular academic disciplines in higher education and an explosion of academic readers and teachers under an obligation to write and publish in their areas of specialism.

The libels, keys, reflections, memoirs and second parts to which Gulliver refers reflect the polemical as well as the opportunistic character of much eighteenth-century book-making. The range of secondary writing has since been extended into other categories and the emphasis has changed, but the critical agenda has throughout the greater part of the book's critical history been determined by the kinds of accusations Gulliver reports and by a tendency to personalise commentary in terms of Swift's own life and personality. This is certainly true of the several memoirs and biographical commentaries which appeared in print after Swift's death in 1745. Indeed, throughout the late eighteenth century and the nineteenth century critics of Swift are much preoccupied with Swift himself and slip incautiously between comments on the text and comments on the author. Though they delight in the sheer accomplishment of Swift's art, what most attracts their attention is the darker and more disturbing side of the satire (especially in the fourth voyage) and, working from their own shocked reactions, they proceed to explain what offends them by reference to what was known or surmised about Swift himself. The biographical obsession remains strong for the first half of this century but to an increasing extent a more detached and scholarly approach begins to be apparent. In critical studies published in the 1950s, for example, one witnesses a concerted effort by academic critics to wrest Swift from the sensationalising biographical interpreters. The emphasis now falls upon the nature and artistry of Swift's satire, upon those rhetorical structures and procedures which can be studied in virtual isolation from biographical considerations. However, satire, the most topical of all the literary kinds, the most tightly embedded in the circumstances of the age which produced it, is not so conveniently studied in pure aesthetic isolation as, say, a lyric, and a great deal of modern criticism of *Gulliver's Travels* is historical in its approach. The justification for this way of looking at the book is self-evident in those parts of the *Travels* which do indeed appear to reflect upon 'great states-folk': most obviously in the political allegory in the first voyage but also in the many passages in which Gulliver reflects and reports upon government and the conduct of political rulers. These invite the identification of actual historical originals and also the kind of commentary which, joining hands with political theory and moral philosophy, relates them to contemporary thought. Once the historical path is followed it soon opens up the book's connections with contemporary science, the voyages of exploration and, more generally, with contemporary views of human nature which (as Gulliver himself complains) the book has persistently been accused of degrading.

This brief survey explains the three emphases I have chosen in this book: (a) Author-centred Approaches in which criticism derives from or refers back to the life and personality of the author; (b) Formal and Rhetorical Approaches in which the focus is upon the book's literary method, and (c) Historical Approaches in which its meaning and significance are explained by reference to political, social and intellectual history. I am conscious that some approaches, more or less valuable, escape this net. All readers owe an often inadequately acknowledged debt to the labours of editors, biographers and annotators who seek to establish the facts of the case (not however without their own differences of opinion) before the critics and interpreters move in. Because Benjamin Motte, the first publisher of the *Travels*, cautiously amended or excised certain passages which were later restored on uncertain authority, even the text of the book remains the subject of an on-going debate, which it is not possible to examine here. In some instances what is offered as 'fact' may be highly debatable. Thus some commentators, adopting what one might call a cryptographic approach, have claimed to interpret the imaginary languages of the *Travels* or have detected hidden significances in the apparent coincidence of the dates of Gulliver's voyages with the ecclesiastical calendar (Morrissey, 1978). It is a reasonable guess that the Lilliputian expression of amazement, 'Hekinah Degul', means 'What in the Devil!' and an intriguing possibility that 'Nardac' should be transliterated 'Ill begot' (Clark, 1953), but at the same time it is impossible not to call to mind Swift's own description of the misguided ingenuity of the 'Anagrammatic Method' (*GT* p.237). A much more fruitful line of enquiry which I have touched upon but insufficiently exemplified is the comparative approach, in which the meaning and method of *Gulliver's Travels* are explored by relating it to other works of literature. Studies of this kind often derive from the search for Swift's sources but even when the demonstration of indebtedness is not at issue (it may indeed be ruled out by chronology), comparative analysis is often illuminating in throwing into relief features of the book which might otherwise not be acknowledged. Thus in his study of Swift W. B. C. Watkins (1939) equates the Yahoos with Hamlet's 'beast that wants discourse of reason' and shows that in its energy and tragic power, *Gulliver's Travels* has much in common with *Hamlet* and *King Lear*. It is unusual to find Swift in Shakespeare's company but to do so is to see his misanthropy in a more generous light. Since both Shakespeare and Swift were Montaigne's inheritors the comparison is not altogether surprising, but in view of Swift's respect for established values it may come as something of a shock to find his name linked with such modern exponents of 'black humour' and the absurd as Samuel Beckett, Norman Mailer and Jean Genet. Yet this line of comparison is fruitful too, for, as Claude Rawson's essays demonstrate, it brings into focus the anarchic tendency of Swift's writings and his boldness in going to extremes in achieving his satirical effects.

Complaining of the bundles delivered to him by the carrier, Gulliver observed that 'the writers. . . are not agreed among themselves'. This has remained the case. Even in so simple a matter as the relative merits of the four parts there are wide divergences of opinion. One critic suggests that the first two voyages are almost perfect, that the third might have been omitted and the fourth toned down; another that it is the fourth and to a less extent the third that command our attention while the reader's interest in the first two is essentially the same as a child's. The third voyage has often been regarded as lacking in unified imaginative power, indeed as an artistic failure, but it, too, has its convincing defenders. Few modern critics would disagree with the view that the fourth voyage is the most powerful part and the key to the whole, but this is a relatively recent view: in the nineteenth century Thackeray advised readers to avoid it and Edmund Gosse suggested that it be banished from 'decent households'. And when in 1923 T. S. Eliot said that he regarded it as 'one of the greatest triumphs that the human soul has ever achieved' he was perhaps directly challenging William A. Eddy, one of the foremost Swift scholars of the day, who in the same year described the voyage as 'unconvincing and unpopular with all but the professional misanthrope' (Eddy, 1923, p.172).

If the critics now agree on the importance of the fourth voyage there is marked disagreement about its interpretation. Less inclined than their predecessors to jump to hostile conclusions, they have looked patiently at the satirical paradigm from every angle. Did Swift actually mean that man is a Yahoo? Is his view of things identical with Gulliver's? Are the Houyhnhnms his ideal? Or are they a satire on Deism? What are we to make of the ending? And what of Pedro de Mendez? James L. Clifford (1974) has reduced the debate to some kind of order by sorting the contributions into two tendencies, 'hard' and 'soft', each of which contains many variants. 'Hard' critics resist those interpretations which accommodate *Gulliver's Travels* to humanistic sensibilities and take the view that for all their unappealing and negative qualities the Houyhnhnms do represent some kind of ideal. 'Soft' critics, on the other hand, suggest that Swift's meaning lies between the two extremes of the Houyhnhnms and the Yahoos and that the former are a false ideal, presented comically, representing attitudes and ideologies of which Swift himself disapproved.

Sampling the contributions to this particular debate, one might be forgiven for thinking that it contains everything that is important about the *Travels*. But to interpret the final voyage is not to interpret the whole work. Because the final voyage deals centrally with overarching questions about human nature and is the climax of the whole book, it may indeed subsume many of the particular issues explored in the earlier parts. Nonetheless overmuch concentration upon the one voyage may leave themes other than the moral nature of man understated. Samuel Holt Monk suggests that the *Travels* is 'a satire on four aspects of man: the physical, the political, the intellectual and the moral': while the first and last of these are particularly strongly represented in the fourth voyage the political and intellectual aspects can only be adequately explored by an examination of the other parts. For some critics the essence of the book is political: thus J. K. Walton (1967) identifies 'the nature of power' as its underlying theme, a view which calls for a more even review of all four voyages. More recently critics such as W. B. Carnochan, F. D. Louis and Everett Zimmerman have emphasised its 'epistemological' aspects, suggesting that in Gulliver we witness 'a man fumbling his way towards knowledge' (Louis, 1981, p.123), which brings into review in fictional form philosophical issues about the nature and perception of reality.

In focusing upon philosophical aspects of language and meaning, the contributions just cited share to some degree the markedly philosophical cast of structuralist and post-structuralist literary theory, which, having called into question received ideas about literature, can now be expected to usher in a new phase in Swift criticism. The works of an author such as Swift who departs from straightforward narratorial strategies and who seems deliberately to set interpretative problems for readers would seem to cry out for the attention of those who insist that literary meaning is inherently problematic. Thus Swift's satirical technique of changing viewpoints in order to defamiliarise the familiar was of particular interest to the Russian Formalists, precursors of recent literary theorists. But, as Edward Said (1984) has made clear, Swift sets problems for those of the avant-garde who deny what commonsense has for generations assumed: that the writer himself is the controlling source of what a text says and that his words are calculated to reflect and to change a real world which exists outside the text.

The value of modern critical perspectives lies in the way it gives a new impetus to existing lines of enquiry. Thus in his ambitious study, *The Discourse of Modernism* (1982), Timothy J. Reiss applies insights drawn from Michel Foucault and other seminal modern theorists to language in *Gulliver's Travels*. At the heart of much recent literary theory is the notion that what we know of the world is predetermined by language, which shapes our consciousness by imposing upon us the values and significances with which it is 'inscribed'. In this view language is not the writer's servant but his master. Without conceding this last point, historical scholarship which calls upon a reading of eighteenth century philosophers carries us in this direction. Reiss takes us further in an illuminating analysis of the language of the Houyhnhnms. As if in exemplification of Wittgenstein's propositions, it appears that the limits of their language are the limits of their world, that they cannot think what they cannot say. But there is a contradiction here: although Gulliver reports that they have no notion of power, government, war, law or punishment, they do in fact use these in the conduct of their affairs. A process of 'occultation' leaves such vicious institutions unacknowledged within their language although they are surreptitiously present in their world.

In another recent study Nigel Wood (1986) endeavours to apply the ideas of Derrida and Foucault to the much-discussed question of Swift's presence in his texts. What is most significant here is that, in dispelling the assumption that the meaning of a literary work ought to be coherent, modern theory reinforces the sense others share that interpretations of the *Travels* should acknowledge that its meaning is elusive, complex and even contradictory.

The most impressive of recent theoretically informed contributions are the essays of Edward Said who deplores the tendency, much in evidence among avant-garde theorists, to close literature off from history and political reality, as if 'textuality' were 'produced by no one and at no time'. He suggests, in effect, that historical and even author-centred approaches still have validity when he asserts that Swift, the most 'worldly' of writers, cannot be divorced from 'the reality of power and authority' and that he 'resists any kind of critical approach that does not make his existence . . . the main avenue to approaching him'. Of particular value is his essay, 'Swift as Intellectual' (a worthy successor to those of Leavis and Orwell), in which he addresses the question: What kind of writer is Swift? In his view Swift should be seen, not as 'a moralist and thinker who peddled one or another final view of human nature' but as 'a kind of local activist', a 'reactive' writer responding to the pressure of immediate historical circumstance. Above all, he argues, Swift assumes the role of the 'intellectual' in the sense that he is one of society's 'keepers of values' whose mission it is 'to tell the truth regardless of material consequences'.

PART ONE: SURVEY

Author-centred approaches

F. R. LEAVIS begins his well-known essay, 'The Irony of Swift' (1934), by insisting that he is dealing not with the man but with the writings. This is a declaration of what he would have regarded as the proper approach to the writings of any author, but in the case of Swift it was all the more necessary because the pressure of critical precedent worked in precisely the opposite direction, making it 'peculiarly difficult', as Leavis acknowledges, to discuss the works 'without shifting the focus of discussion to the kind of man Swift was'. Throughout the eighteenth and nineteenth centuries literary works were so often considered within a biographical framework (in, for example, Dr Johnson's *Lives of the Poets*, 1779–81, and John Morley's English Men of Letters series) that a 'writer and his works' approach came to be the staple form of literary criticism. This was reinforced by the view, associated with Romanticism, which held sway throughout the nineteenth century, that literature is above all an expression and embodiment of the individual writer's consciousness. Susan Sontag sums this up when she says 'the Romantic and post-Romantic sensibility discerns in every book a first-person performance' (1982, p.xv). It was in reaction against this view that T. S. Eliot developed what he called his 'Impersonal theory' of poetry ('not the expression of personality, but an escape from personality') and thus helped to establish a new orthodoxy for the twentieth century, the orthodoxy which Leavis affirms, in which the central focus is emphatically the text and not the author. (See Eliot's essay 'Tradition and the Individual Talent', 1919.)

Swift proved the most intractable of authors in this regard: so pervasive was his felt presence in his works and so closely, seemingly, was his personality involved in the most disturbing and controversial aspects of his writings that a kind of slippage towards the biographical, and subsequently the psychoanalytical, seemed irresistible. Despite emphatic disclaimers ('Here, well on the side of pathology, literary criticism stops.') Leavis himself does not entirely overcome the temptation when he concludes that 'Swift is distinguished by the intensity of his feelings, not by insight into them, and he certainly does not impress us as a mind in possession of his experience'. This is more, I think, than the familiar substitution of an author's name for his writings (we say we read 'Shakespeare'); it is a reminder of how deeply engrained in our literary tradition is the habit of reading a work of literature as the expression of its author's personality.

Writing in 1934, Leavis may have recalled a relatively recent discussion of Swift which failed to stop this side of pathology: Aldous Huxley's colourful and tendentious essay published in the collection *Do What You Will* (1928). Taking as his starting point Swift's casual remark, 'I hate the word bowels', Huxley presents a portrait, with much supporting reference to the scatalogical poems and the mystery of Swift's intimate but presumably unconsummated relationship with Stella Johnson, of a man incapable of physical love and thus prevented from growing to full human maturity. In the strict sense Huxley was not writing literary criticism at all, but his principal references to *Gulliver's Travels* are significant. He says the Yahoos were *Swift's* (not simply Gulliver's) 'personal enemies', 'chiefly because they smelt of sweat and excrement, because they had genital organs and dugs, groins and hairy armpits; their moral shortcomings were of secondary importance'. And he discovers in the *Travels* a refusal 'to accept the physical reality of the world'. In its display of psychological sophistication Huxley's portrayal is distinctively 'modern', but his materials and his insistence on the conjoining of the personal and the literary are traditional features of Swift criticism.

The Irish poet W. B. Yeats (1865–1939) was so conscious of Swift as a living presence that he said of his fellow Dubliner, 'Swift haunts me: he is always just round the next corner'. He discerned the key to Swift in the suggestions that he feared madness and was indeed incipiently mad even before he sank into a state of senile dementia in old age. He drew upon some of these details in his play *The Words upon the Window-pane* (1934).

A group of spiritualists gather for a seance in a Dublin house formerly occupied by Stella Johnson. The proceedings begin but are then disrupted by the presence of Swift's malign spirit, whom we hear in agonised conversation with Stella, rejecting her plea that he marry her: 'I have something in my blood that no child must inherit'. But Yeats offers another dimension to Swift's madness: it is the madness of the intellect itself, induced by a visionary prospect of the collapse of the social order during the French Revolution at the end of the century. Recalling some of the heroic figures conjured upon in Glubbdubdribb (p.241) the young Cambridge scholar John Corbet remarks in the play:

> His ideal order was the Roman Senate, his ideal men Brutus and Cato. Such an order and such men had seemed possible once more, but the movement passed and he foresaw the ruin to come, Democracy, Rousseau, the French Revolution; that is why he hated the common run of men, ... that is why he wrote *Gulliver*, that is why he wore out his brain, that is why he felt *saeva indignatio* ...

Behind Huxley and Yeats lie innumerable comments on Swift which in a similar way deploy inferences about his personality and personal life. Many of them are to be found in the flood of posthumous recollection and comment which helped to fix the portrait of the morose and frustrated genius conjured up nearly two centuries later in Yeats's play. This is the Swift we know from Dr Johnson's *Life* (1781): 'not a man to be either loved or envied [who] seems to have wasted life in discontent by the rage of neglected pride' and who from 'depravity of intellect ... took delight in revolving ideas from which almost every other mind shrinks with disgust'.

Initial reactions to *Gulliver's Travels* appear to have been predominantly favourable. The most famous reports of its reception are from Swift's friends, but even allowing for favouritism it is clear that it was a publishing sensation ('It has been the conversation of the whole town', John Gay reported; 'from the highest to the lowest it is universally read, from the Cabinet Council to the Nursery'). Then as now the sheer imaginative ingenuity of the book ('invention' was the apt eighteenth-century word) took hold of readers' imaginations: 'The Duchess Dowager of Marlborough is in raptures at it; she says she can dream of nothing else since she read it' (*Casebook*, p.30). And its appeal was further spiced by the need to guess the identity of the author.

Swift clearly regarded his book as politically sensitive and expected repercussions from the government – hence the arrangement for the *Travels* to be published in London, without any public acknowledgement of his authorship, after he had returned to Ireland. Indeed it was occasionally depicted as a seditious work, but what proved more strongly and enduringly controversial was its unflattering portrayal of human nature. John Gay reported that some readers found it impious and 'an insult on providence' and the author of the anonymous 'Letter from a Clergyman to his Friend' (1726) amplifies the reasons for such a reaction. He expresses disgust at the fourth voyage: 'Tis with the utmost Pain a generous Mind must endure the Recital; A Man grows sick at the shocking things inserted there; his Gorge rises; he is not able to conceal his Resentment; and closes the book with Detestation and Disappointment.' He then turns the attack upon Swift himself: 'Here, Sir, you may see a reverend Divine, a dignify'd member of the Church unbosoming himself, unloading his Breast, discovering the true Temper of his Soul, drawing his own Picture to the Life . . . Here's the most inveterate Rancour of his Mind, and a hoard of Malice, twelve years collecting, discharged at one; Here's ENVY, the worst of all Passions, in Perfection; ENVY, the most beloved Darling of Hell; the greatest Abhorrence of Heaven' (Williams, 1970, p.67).

This kind of two-pronged attack is to be found in several of the remarks, memoirs and critical biographies published soon after Swift's death in 1745, in quoting from which I have used Kathleen Williams's collection of early Swift criticism in the 'Critical Heritage' series (1970). It is occasioned by a genuine revulsion at the satirical use of gross physical imagery, in particular at its religious implications and the cast of mind which it seems to imply. In part at least it reflects also the prevalence of a more benevolent view of human nature and increasing alienation from hard-hitting satire. Appropriately enough in 1748 we find Samuel Richardson, whose novels exemplify the new accent upon refined feeling in a peculiarly insistent form, reporting in fiction that his heroine, Clarissa, 'often pitied the celebrated Dr. Swift for so employing his admirable pen, that a pure eye was afraid of looking into his works and a pure ear of hearing any thing quoted from them' (p.104). Such objections applied to a whole range of Swift's writings but in the case of *Gulliver's Travels*, while unease is expressed at various incidental indelicacies, it is the fourth voyage which chiefly offends. Lord Orrery (1752) sees the voyage as 'a real insult upon mankind' and objects both to the Yahoos ('In painting YAHOOS he becomes one himself') and to the cold insipidity of the Houyhnhnms (p.127). In Patrick Delaney's view both the Yahoos and the Houyhnhnms are in their different ways a debasement of mankind and thus of God's handiwork. He vindicates mankind against Swift's description by drawing attention to the 'amazing powers, with which God has endowed the human frame' and, by ridiculing the Houyhnhnms' limitations and inadequacies, endeavours to show that they are in no way superior to mankind (1754, pp.132–5). Edward Young (1759), expressing a similar view, finds further grounds for offence in the fact that the Son of God took human form: thus Swift 'has blasphemed a nature little lower than that of angels, and assumed by far higher than they' (p.179).

What was unpalatable to Young, Delaney, Richardson and Orrery might only a few decades previously have been regarded as an acceptable way of underlining the deficiencies of human nature and the need for Christian redemption. Although this tradition was in decline, Swift did not lack defenders who recognised what he was doing and approved of it. For example, John Wesley in a sermon on original sin quotes extensively and approvingly Swift's denunciations of warfare in the second and fourth voyages. Writing in 1755 John Hawkesworth answers the attacks directly: 'Let not him be censured for too much debasing his species, who has contributed to their felicity and preservation by stripping off the veil of custom and prejudice, and holding up in their native deformity the vices by which they became wretched, and the arts by which they are destroyed (Williams, 1970, pp.153–4). In the same year Deane Swift (Swift's nephew) asks why, if we praise 'that excellent moralist, the humorous Hogarth' for exposing vices and follies in his satirical drawings, should 'we condemn a preacher of righteousness, for exposing under the character of a nasty unteachable YAHOO the deformity, the blackness, the filthiness and corruption of those hellish, abominable vices, which inflame the wrath of GOD against the children of disobedience?' (p.144). Deane Swift provides the answer to Young: Swift's methods are justified and his view of human nature consistent with a Christian view of fallen man wallowing in sin: 'That glorious creature man, is deservedly more contemptible than a brute beast, when he flies in the face of his CREATOR . . . And this manifestly appears to be the groundwork of the whole satire contained in the voyage to the HOUYHNHNMS' (p.145).

The most considered eighteenth-century defence is Thomas Sheridan's (1784) who argues that *Gulliver's Travels* has been completely misinterpreted. Swift's intention was not to debase human nature but to show the way in which mankind could attain true dignity. What is particularly interesting in his account is his explanation of Swift's strategy in constructing a fable which separates two partial and complementary aspects of Man, represented by the Yahoos and the Houyhnhnms, in order to show that one should not have absolute command over the other. 'In your merely animal capacity, says he to man, without reason to guide you, and actuated only by a blind instinct, I will show you that you would be degraded below the beasts of the field. . . . On the other hand, I will show another picture of an animal endowed with a rational soul, and acting uniformly up to the dictates of right reason. Here you may see collected all the virtues, all the great qualities, which dignify man's nature, and constitute the happiness of his life' (pp.236–7). As if further to neutralise objections to the Yahoos, Sheridan discovers a number of points of difference between them and humankind (squirrel-like nimbleness, the formation and strength of their nails), while claiming elsewhere that they are no worse than the most primitive races or a wild degenerate discovered in the woods.

Sheridan was aware that the weight of opinion was against him and we can now see that the arguments of those who defended Swift were not generally adopted. In spite of an eminently balanced contribution from William Hazlitt (1818, *Casebook*, pp.55–7) the complaints of madness, misanthropy and gross offensiveness ran on into the nineteenth century, rising to the crescendo of W. M. Thackeray's startling attack (1851): 'a monster gibbering shrieks and gnashing imprecations against mankind – tearing down all shreds of modesty, past all sense of manliness and shame; filthy in word, filthy in thought, furious, raging, obscene' (*Casebook*, p.60). For Thackeray, like many of his predecessors, the next step is to seek an explanatory cause in Swift himself: 'What had this man done? What secret remorse was rankling at his heart? What fever was boiling in him, that he should see all the world bloodshot?' The same association between unacceptably shocking satire and the disordered personality of the author is developed later in the nineteenth century by Leslie Stephen. But whereas Thackeray imagines Swift harbouring a dark and guilty secret like a Gothic villain, for Stephen it becomes a matter which invites medical and psychological explanation rather than moral condemnation: 'His indulgence in revolting images is to some extent an indication of a diseased condition of his mind, perhaps of actual mental decay' (Stephen, 1882, p.180). He remarks on the paradox that Swift combined personal fastidiousness verging on prudery with a preoccupation with filth and likens his state of mind to those religious ascetics who 'stimulate their contempt for the flesh by fixing their gaze upon decaying bodies'. Stephen's view of Swift is a complex one in which judgement is tempered by sympathy and an appreciation of his achievements: 'Some of us . . . rather pity than condemn the wounded spirit so tortured and perverted, in consideration of the real philanthropy which underlies the misanthropy, and the righteous hatred of brutality and oppression which is but the seamy side of a generous sympathy' (pp.184–5). This is a considerable advance on the noisy moral outrage of Thackeray for it offers a way into the complexity of the text rather than a reason for not reading it.

The personal emphasis remained strong in Swift criticism until the 1950s. Like Huxley, George Orwell, writing in 1946, is convinced of the inadequacy of the world-view projected in *Gulliver's Travels* and traces its origins to the notion that 'Swift is a diseased writer' (Orwell, 1970, p.259). R. M. Adams's discussion now seems dated in its assumption (which Orwell shares) that the Houyhnhnms are Swift's unequivocal ideal but it conveys strongly a sense of an author so deeply committed to satire as not merely to lacerate his reader's feelings but to court the destruction of his own mental stability (Donoghue, 1971). Bonamy Dobrée, who insists that the *Travels* is 'a healthy book', emphasises not disorder but emotional complexity as the distinguishing feature of the book's personal dimension. Echoing Pope's lines in *The Dunciad* he says: 'So much of Swift is here; not Gulliver alone, but Dean, Drapier, Bickerstaff, by turns choosing Cervantes' serious air, or shaking with Rabelaisian laughter; the rounded man is before you, in movement, varying in mood and in response, with all the surprises of a living human being, with the gaiety and the tragedy of a great one' (Dobrée, 1959, p.447).

We have already seen that Huxley (1929) brings psychology to bear upon Swift. In this he evidently follows Leslie Stephen's lead, even to the extent of developing Stephen's point about religious ascetics with some characteristically erudite parallels from the lives of Mme Guyon and St Francis of Assisi. And in turn Huxley foreshadows the application of psychoanalysis to Swift criticism. John Middleton Murry (1954) pursues what he calls 'the personal equation' by arguing that Swift's early circumstances bred in him a deep distrust of a 'love-marriage' and 'a deliberate and prolonged repression of the emotion of love' leading to extreme loathing of the physical and sexual functions. Consequently, when Murry contemplates Gulliver's encounter with the young female Yahoo, he finds it 'impossible to suppress the notion that Swift is annihilating Stella herself as a sexual being . . . cauterizing . . . the possibility of a sexual relation with her' (pp.351–4). A more extreme account is given by Phyllis Greenacre (1955) who detects a series of interconnections between Swift's personality and *Gulliver's Travels*. The misadventures of Swift's early years figure prominently: his lack of a father, the enforced separation from his mother, the rigours of his toilet training and his relations with Jane Waring, Vanessa and Stella, as well as the resultant personality traits. In her reading of *Gulliver's Travels*, reminiscences of these and other formative experiences abound. Gulliver's accounts of toilet facilities and emergencies resemble the dilemmas of a child trying to be good by performing his toilet functions in the right place at the right time, but getting a secret satisfaction through irregularities of performance. The description of the Lilliputian educational system, in which children are separated from parents and in which sexual difference is minimised, is seen as 'a satirical attack on Swift's own early life'. The abduction of Gulliver by the monkey (II.v. 161–2) recalls the fact that Swift was kidnapped by his nurse at the age of one, while the calling up of great men from the past is possibly the recalling and overcoming of the dead father. Greenacre also detects voyeurism, masturbation ('Master Bates' and pervasively in the rising and falling of the Flying Island), a homosexual fellatio fantasy (the monkey stuffing Gulliver's mouth) and, in changes in body size, a preoccupation with phallic functioning.

J. M. Murry gave one of his chapters the title 'The Excremental Vision' and it is this phrase which Norman O. Brown

(Tuveson, 1964) adopts as the title of a lively and combative essay in which he contests the validity of many psychoanalytical interpretations. Brown does not attempt to play down the importance of the excremental theme and indeed is impatient with those who attempt to do so, but he is equally hard upon those psychoanalysts who, in effect, judge Swift to be insane. His well-chosen quotations reveal the extremes to which psychoanalytical interpretations have gone in detecting signs of neurosis, psychosexual infantilism, coprophilia, mysogyny, misanthropy, mysophilia and mysophobia. Brown turns such arguments on their head, first by reminding his readers that what the critics and psychoanalysts discover in Swift is only his individual version of a universal human neurosis which they themselves share and then by proceeding to argue that in his emphasis upon anality and sublimation Swift actually anticipates Freud: 'The excremental vision of the Yahoo is substantially identical with the psychoanalytical doctrine of the extensive role of anal erotism in the formation of human culture' (p.43). Thus the *Travels* and Swift's other satires are seen not as materials for a case study in abnormality but as vehicles for a vision of human activity and motivation which the uncomfortable insights of modern pyschoanalysis confirm and validate.

Brown's critique of psychoanalytical approaches coincided in time with an emphasis upon text, form and genre, an approach which consciously eschews the investigation of the personality of the author. In this light earlier biographical and psychological interpretations of *Gulliver's Travels* may seem crudely literal, especially in confusing Gulliver with his creator. Nonetheless a recognition that the book bears the distinctively personal imprint of its author still persists and recent criticism seeks to account for this in ways which avoid both the heavy-handedness of earlier moralistic and post-war psychoanalytic commentators and the convenient simplicity of assuming a complete separation between Gulliver and his creator. The most distinguished criticism of this kind comes from C. J. Rawson whose essay 'Gulliver and the Gentle Reader' (Rawson, 1973) includes sensitive but not easily summarised comments on ways in which, while Gulliver 'is not identical with Swift, nor even similar to him, . . . Swift's presence behind him is always too close to ignore'. As an example Rawson recalls Gulliver's embarrassment when forced by necessity to relieve himself in his

Lilliputian house and his insistence upon his 'cleanliness' in the face of what 'maligners' have said to the contrary, and observes: 'It is Gulliver and not Swift who is speaking, but it is Swift and not Gulliver who . . . has had maligners'. The precision of Rawson's distinction is significant for it recognises the rhetorical separation of author and persona without denying the author's personal emotional and ideological investment in the text.

The critical biography remains one of the staple genres of Swift studies and modern readers are fortunate to have at their disposal recent publications of this kind by Irvin Ehrenpreis (1962–83), J.A. Downie (1984) and David Nokes (1985), all of which offer well-balanced accounts of the man and the works.

Formal and rhetorical approaches

In *The Cankered Muse*, a study of satire published in 1959, Alvin Kernan blames biographical and historical methods of criticism for some of the misunderstandings which surround satire. He deplores the way in which these approaches deny satirical works the autonomy of a work of art and cause criticism to 'degenerate into discussion of an author's moral character and the economic and social conditions of his time'. As an alternative he suggests that we should consider the satirical works as 'a construct of symbols – situations, scenes, character, language – put together to express some particular vision of the world' and adds: 'The individual parts must be seen in terms of their function in the total poem and not judged by reference to things outside the poem such as the medical history of the author or the social scene in which he wrote'. This is an important statement and one that is particularly pertinent to the present study because, in justifying his preferred method, Kernan denounces both of the other approaches we have identified for consideration.

Kernan's attitude reflects the state of criticism at the time he was writing both in its determination to resist the pull towards the biographical and in its concern to develop an adequate method of dealing analytically with the formal and rhetorical elements of the literary work. It would be easy to suggest that any kind of artistic construct which has been composed to express a particular vision of the world can hardly be isolated from whatever in that world determined the nature of that vision, but the determination to consider literature purely as literature was widely shared at the time Kernan was writing and produced analytical insights which still have value today.

Genre–a novel?

To assign a work of literature to its genre might appear to be a straightforward task to be undertaken as a preliminary to further formal analysis. But in the case of *Gulliver's Travels* it proves to be peculiarly difficult. When it first appeared, the novel as we now know it was in its infancy and, indeed, the term 'novel' was not available with its modern meaning. But even when, later in the century, the terms 'novel' and 'romance' were both in use it would not have been immediately obvious which should be applied to the *Travels*. While it has, in the nature and locations of Gulliver's adventures, the improbability of romance, it has in its narrative manner the realism of the novel such, indeed, 'as to deceive us into a persuasion (at least while we are reading) that all is real'. (The quotation is from Clara Reeve's distinction between the novel and the romance; see M. Allott (ed.), *Novelists on the Novel*, 1959, p.47.)

Most modern readers would have little hesitation in referring to *Gulliver's Travels*, as they would to Daniel Defoe's *Robinson Crusoe*, as a novel; professional critics might not agree. Walter Allen, for example, is quite emphatic: 'though possessing many of the attributes of a novelist [Swift] cannot be called one' and '*Gulliver's Travels* is a work of fiction but not a novel' (Allen, 1954).

Although the experiments of modern novelists are calling into question received assumptions about the nature of the form, it is still a common expectation that the novel will exhibit two features which distinguished it from earlier forms of fiction – individualised characters presented in a realistic setting. In Arnold Kettle's view individualisation is notably lacking from the *Travels*: 'though he is a convincing enough figure for Swift's purposes, [Gulliver] has no existence of his own'. And it is because the author's primary interests lie elsewhere that he regards the *Travels* as a 'moral fable' rather than a novel. He explains the difference in this way: whereas the novel starts with life itself and is essentially concerned with 'moral discovery', the author of a moral fable 'starts with his pattern, his moral vision, and . . . the various elements of the novel, character and plot in particular, are consciously subordinated to and in a special sense derived from the pattern' (Kettle, 1954, p.17).

Ronald Paulson (1967) sets up similar dichotomies: between the novel, 'a form interested in human experience for its own sake' and satire, a form 'that advocated strict moral judgement'; between the novel with its organic conception of character as personality enduring through time, developing, maturing, decaying, dying, and satire's judicial use of character to make a satiric point. Frederick R. Karl calls the *Travels* a 'near-novel' (Kettle's term) for similar reasons. It depends upon general principles rather than the nature of experience and inevitably therefore Gulliver lacks 'inner life'. Thus although *Robinson Crusoe* and *Gulliver's Travels* both belong to 'that genre of prose narrative involving travel, shipwreck, abandonment, exotic adventures, strung-together episodes' and although Gulliver's attitudes and situations resemble Crusoe's, Defoe's book is a novel and Swift's is not (Karl, 1974, pp.279–81).

Gulliver—a defective hero?

Essential to each of these accounts is the way in which Gulliver is presented. The charge is that Swift sacrifices his individuality to the over-riding requirements of satirical effect. Other critics forcefully underline this point. Denis Donoghue says that it is irrelevant to talk of Gulliver's character: 'He has no character, he is a cipher . . .. He is what he does, what we see him doing, there is nothing beyond what we see . . .. Gulliver carries nothing from one occasion to another; with every voyage he starts again: no memories, no experience, no character. We are not invited to care what happens to him, as we care what happens to Moll Flanders' (Donoghue, 1969, p.162). Donoghue is perhaps a little more categorical than the facts warrant (Gulliver does carry memories – of his family, previous adventures and earlier life – lacking in prominence though these may be), but what he draws attention to is the limited extent to which Swift explores the consciousness of Gulliver as Defoe would have done. To some degree this limitation may be a function of the kind of man Gulliver is (and many critics take Gulliver's character as given and discuss his deficiencies as personal shortcomings rather than artistic imperfections). Undoubtedly it is also a result of the kind of artistic function he has to perform. R. C. Elliott notes the same kind of missing characteristics: 'Gulliver's is a life without nuance'; 'he has the most minimal subjective life'; 'he is, in fact, an abstraction, manipulated in the service of satire'. He goes on to illustrate the kind of inconsistency which results from this by drawing attention to Gulliver's refusal to bring a free people into slavery in the first voyage and his contradictory suggestion to the king in the second voyage that he use gunpowder to keep his people in subjection (Elliott, 1960, p.200).

Satirical forms

When Elliott follows his depiction of Gulliver as a satirical mouthpiece with this remark – 'To say this of the principal character of a novel would be damning; but to say this of a work written according to the conventions of Lucian's *A True Story*, the *Satyricon*, *Gargantua* is simply to describe' – he is offering an answer to the inevitable question: if *Gulliver's Travels* is not a novel then what is it?

The writings of Lucian, Petronius and Rabelais to which Elliott refers are very different in kind and it is therefore not immediately clear what they and the *Travels* have in common. In what sense do they constitute a common and coherent tradition? Studies of literary genre in the 1950s and 1960s, and in particular of the nature of satire, help to provide an answer. They correct the common view that satire is primarily about attack and draw attention to the derivation of 'satire' from *satura lanx* (Latin for 'a well-filled dish'), which suggests a medley or miscellaneous variety of fare. This gives a clue which several critics have followed in showing that the *Travels* is written in a tradition which values variety and a free inclusiveness as well as a playful and irreverent way of addressing its subject matter. Northrop Frye applied the term 'Menippean satire' to fictions of this kind. He describes its subject matter as being mental attitudes rather than people, types (pedants, cranks, parvenus, virtuosi) rather than individuals. Its stylised characters are used as mouthpieces for the ideas they represent and its narrative form is loose and accommodating. However it may take a more concentrated form and present 'a vision of the world in terms of a single intellectual pattern' (Frye, 1957, p.310).

Alvin Kernan's (1959) aims and method are similar: to discern what is quintessential in satire and the satiric vision of life in order to arrive at a description which has general validity. Using terms that have strong associations with dramatic structure, he organises his descriptions under three heads: scene, plot and character. His description of the typical satirical scene may call to mind the kind of urban set-piece found in the poems of Pope or Juvenal or in Hogarth's pictures. It is a disorderly scene, densely crowded with deformed, staring faces expressive of a whole range of vices and follies. In its own way *Gulliver's Travels* presents equivalents to this kind of kaleidoscopic survey – in its sweeping inventories of human folly, its set-pieces such as the Academy of Lagado and in its cumulative impact. Kernan's characterisation of the typical stance of the satirist more obviously applies to the *Travels* and, interestingly enough, provides an alternative rationale for the plain style. Although in reality the satirist is subtle and clever in using language, he usually presents himself as a down-to-earth, straightforward fellow who is distinguished by his honest bluntness. Kernan also comments interestingly on the satiric plot. The word 'plot' is usually taken to mean 'what happens' but in satire 'we seem at the conclusion . . . to be always at very nearly the same point where we began'. As if to answer the objection that indeed Gulliver changes, that he and his vision are not the same in Lilliput as after his return from Houyhnhnmland, Kernan adds that instead of change we witness the intensification of the initial situation. In this, he argues, satire differs from tragedy, in which the hero gains a new and truer recognition of the nature of the world and the evil within it, which then provides the basis for a new purpose. Whether in the light of this we should see the end of *Gulliver's Travels* as moving towards tragedy or as a burlesque of tragedy is left open to question.

To assign the *Travels* to so loose a form as Menippean satire is to leave open other generic possibilities. It finds its place, naturally enough, in P. B. Gove's authoritative check-list in *The Imaginary Voyage in Prose Fiction* (1941). Struck by the book's strong content of ideas, some critics have discerned its true affinities to lie with works of a philosophical kind. A. E. Case (1945), calls it 'a politico-sociological treatise much of which is couched in the medium of satire' and Carnochan (1968) mentions a number of possibilities, among them a 'satirical essay on man'. Ellen Douglass Leyburn considers it as Satiric Allegory in a book with that title (1956). Others find terms to indicate the flexibility and open-endedness of its form: Peter Steele (1978) speaks of its 'exploratory form' and Denis Donoghue of its belonging to the 'plural form' which gives Swift the freedom 'to do whatever he chooses when the humour takes him', to 'introduce anything he wants, when he wants it; taking his material from any convenient source'. As an example, Donoghue shows that when the King of Brobdingnag is critical of England's 'chargeable and extensive wars' (*GT* p.171) he expresses the author's own views, Swift's principal concern being to 'have the reader meet these sentiments at this moment'. This kind of freedom necessarily poses problems for the reader and Donoghue warns that 'in plural form we have to accustom ourselves to live from moment to moment' (Donoghue, 1971, pp.15–16).

Lemuel Gulliver – character, author or rhetorical device?

We are now perhaps in a position to take the discussion of Lemuel Gulliver beyond the point of denying him the status of a character in a novel in the realist tradition. Discussion of his fictional status and satirical function can be seen as an attempt to steer a course between extremes. He may, as in author-centred approaches, be regarded as his creator's *alter ego*, the spokesman of Swift's conscious opinions and the betrayer of his prejudices and unconscious impulses. He may on the other hand be presented as a consciously manipulated device distanced from Swift's own viewpoint and used, indeed, to represent what Swift himself abhorred. Only occasionally is either view developed to the point at which it totally excludes the other: the needle of critical opinion tends to settle, though with a good deal of wavering, between the two extremes. That is to say, Gulliver is seen as Swift's spokesman *and* his satirical butt, as a self-projection *and* an embodiment of what he wished to ridicule. That we make sense of these apparent contradictions is the result of learning, in Donoghue's terms, to live from moment to moment as we read the *Travels*.

Essential to the modern understanding of Gulliver's role is a relatively recent critical invention – the concept of the 'persona' or 'mask'. This, as R. C. Elliott shows in his admirable study of the subject (*The Literary Persona*, 1982), has been widely used in literary criticism as a way of differentiating between the author and the voice or pose he adopts when writing in the first person. Elliott sees the concept as originating with G. L. Kittredge's distinction in a discussion of *The Book of the Duchess* between the author (Chaucer) and the 'I' of the poem (the Dreamer), the latter being 'a purely imaginary figure, to whom certain purely imaginary things happen, in a purely imaginary dream'. As Elliott suggests, the notion of distinguishing in this way between author and persona coincided with and gained strength from the recognition that we encounter a similar distinction in modernist poetry, as between T. S. Eliot and his J. Alfred Prufrock or between Ezra Pound and his Hugh Selwyn Mauberley, for example. The concept was not extensively adopted into literary criticism until after the Second World War. It was at this stage that it proved to be of particular value in the discussion of Swift (and also of Pope) to those critics who had become increasingly impatient with the persistent tendency to adopt personal interpretations of his writings. The misreading of *Gulliver's Travels* as the personal expression of one man's grudge against the world was seen in large part to result from the simplistic identification of Swift with Gulliver, as instanced by Carl van Doren's words: 'Swift would have remained with the Houyhnhnms for ever if they had not sent him away'. And persona theory offered the solution.

It made it possible to show that in satires such as *A Modest Proposal* and *A Tale of a Tub* Swift's habitual practice was to act a part, to impersonate a speaker who, even when anonymous and not supplied with a full set of biographical particulars, was felt to be someone other than Swift. Lemuel Gulliver could thus be explained as a further extension of this practice. The main advantage was that, in separating Gulliver from Swift, discussion was freed from the obsession with the author's personality. At the same time, the term 'persona' proved to be useful in encapsulating the ways in which Gulliver differed from a character in a realist novel. His inconsistencies, for example, need no longer be regarded as deficiencies but as the kind of liberties a satirist would be expected to take with his own equivalent to a ventriloquist's dummy. Gulliver's status was no longer defined in terms of what he lacked by comparison with Robinson Crusoe and Moll Flanders (let alone David Copperfield or Stephen Dedalus); as a persona he was a member of a quite different tradition.

Earlier critics were certainly alive to Gulliver's distinctiveness as a voice or a presence and to Swift's creative and manipulative skill in the use of what we have come to call a persona. Sir Walter Scott praises Swift for his 'power of adopting and sustaining a fictitious character, under every peculiarity of place and circumstance' (Williams, I, 1968, p.154). De Quincey (1847), very significantly, sees Gulliver's individuality as being created through Gulliver's style: it is, he says, 'purposely touched slightly with that dullness of circumstantiality which besets the excellent, but somewhat dull race of men, old sea-captains' (Jordan, 1973, p.314). George Saintsbury (1916) credits Swift with 'some of the highest qualities necessary to the dramatist' (though not detachment from his subject) and John B. More as early as 1928 gave several reasons for his assertion 'that Gulliver is not Swift himself in either intellect or disposition is abundantly clear' (Foster, 1961, p.95).

So far as the study of Swift is concerned two key contributions are Ricardo Quintana's essay 'Situational Satire: A Commentary on the Method of Swift' (1948, reprinted in Tuveson, 1964) and Maynard Mack's 'The Muse of Satire' (1951, reprinted in Paulson, 1971). Both reflect the contemporary emphasis upon impersonality and the desire to release satire from an author-centred emphasis. Quintana draws attention to our ready acceptance of the impersonality of drama ('we do not confuse the dramatist with his characters . . . we do not take the play as direct expression of the writer's personality') and regrets that readers find it so difficult with satire, as with lyric poetry, to see the literary work as an aesthetic construct. The analysis of Swift's satirical method which follows gives a key place to the persona: Quintana describes it as 'dramatic satire', the creation of 'a fully realised character and a fully realised world for him to move in'. He goes so far as to say at one point that Swift is not present and the character is in charge, although he modifies this view later in the essay by suggesting that the author is present but at a distance – 'he stands several levels away'.

Mack argues that the modern rediscovery of rhetoric offers a way of moving the discussion of satire on from the nineteenth century's personalised approaches. His illustrations are drawn from Pope who, writing bitingly in the first person, had often been the subject of highly personalised critical denunciation, but Mack's general formulations (as well as a very pertinent aside on the fourth voyage of the *Travels*) are relevant here. He invites us to consider satire both as a rhetorical construct, as something made, and as exhibiting 'an appreciable degree of fictionality'. For both these reasons it is not the basis upon which we can safely or properly make inferences about the author's state of mind. In so far as the author is present it is author as writer, not the author as man, and what is revealed is in part determined by the genre in which he is working. In the case of Pope he suggests that the genre leads him to revert repeatedly to three satirical stances – of the plain man, the *ingenu* or the public defender. These ideas were subsequently absorbed and elaborated, notably by Alvin Kernan who discovers in satires ancient and modern 'the same proud, fiery, intolerant, irascible man whom no one would want as a neighbour' who takes pride in his plain speaking, his humble origins and his championship of virtue in a degenerating world. The possible applications of this description to Gulliver – at least the Gulliver of the final voyage – will be obvious. And if, indeed, 'the satirist is always an amalgamation of the basic characteristics which develop whenever satire is written', then the objectionable features of Gulliver's vision may be as much a product of the nature and traditions of satire as of the allegedly diseased and misanthropic outlook of Swift himself. What the outraged earlier critics of Swift are therefore objecting to is satire itself.

In presenting a book-length treatment of the subject a few years after Mack's essay William B. Ewald's *The Masks of Jonathan Swift* (1954) signalled that the idea of the persona had arrived. Ewald devotes two chapters to an account of Gulliver's character and adventures and indicates his dual role as 'explainer' and also as 'object' of Swift's satirical message in illustrating by his own example the faults of travel-writers, Englishmen and human beings generally. Ewald's Gulliver is a solidly realised character but considerably less complex and problematic, and perhaps more likeable than he has come to seem. Certain aspects which Ewald acknowledged but perhaps underemphasised have subsequently received a good deal of attention: the change in his outlook, his lack of insight, the extent to which much of the satire is directed against him, the tenuousness of his characterisation, the inconsistencies which result from Swift's manipulation of him, and the frequent intrusion of Swift's own voice.

In one of the most striking analyses Robert C. Elliott focuses upon the paradox that whereas the book is to be taken as if all four voyages were written by Gulliver after his return from Houyhnhnmland, there is no sign (except in the introductory letter added later) of the peculiar vision induced by his contacts with the horses and the Yahoos until we reach the final voyage itself. Thus Elliott distinguishes two Gullivers – 'Gulliver-author, the misanthrope who sits down to tell his tale of woe' and 'the younger Gulliver, the naïve seaman' created by Gulliver-author. As an author Gulliver 'tried hard to keep his mature point of view out of the early voyages, to project himself as a character as he in fact was in time past . . . and to create the illusion of the immediacy of the younger Gulliver's experience'. Although the response of readers over two centuries suggests that he was successful, Swift was by the Jamesian standards widely current when Elliott wrote his essay brought up against the limitations of his form. To do justice to the complex inter-relationship of past and present points of view Swift would have needed to write a psychological novel. Elliott goes on to examine the kinds of inconsistencies which result from the dual viewpoint. In the final voyage Gulliver-author and Gulliver-character become one and there, by his failure to understand the significance of Don Pedro, Gulliver is seen to be committed to a shallow and single-minded vision which distinguishes him from his creator: 'with magnificent unconscious irony he damns himself, and in so doing measures the distance between the shallowness of his insight into the human condition and the great complexity of insight which is Swift's' (Elliott, 1952, p.63).

Critics have come to see that the reaction against the older identification of Gulliver with Swift may have gone too far, that the creation of a rigid distinction between persona and author is, in its own way, a misrepresentation of the text. The most striking evidence of this trend comes from Irvin Ehrenpreis, who has challenged the validity of the persona as a critical concept by insisting that it is in reality a version of the author's voice and not another person's. He draws an analogy with everyday conversation: 'when an intelligent friend suddenly utters absurdities in a sober tone, we do not conclude that he has changed his identity but that he is using dead-pan irony. If his wit grows so mocking that he seems to be imitating a particular fool or type of fool, we do not imagine that he has been metamorphosed' (Ehrenpreis, 1963, p.36). This is a useful reminder, although it may be noticed that the imitation of a particular fool could easily be formalised into a dramatic impersonation, a line of thought which would eventually lead us back to the persona. Another way of correcting the tendency comfortably to insulate the author from his own possibly objectionable meanings by erecting a solid persona as a screen is to point to the psychological strangeness and danger of impersonation. Thus in a later essay Ehrenpreis notes that Swift 'loves to speak in parody of people he detests' and takes on 'in fantasy the very role of the character he means to attack' (Vickers, 1968, p.216). When applied to Gulliver's encounters with the lascivious female Yahoo or with the Brobdingnagian maids of honour the idea of enacting in fantasy may suggest a strange mingling of abhorrence and fascination which leads back to psychoanalytical readings of these episodes. While avoiding the excesses of criticism of this type, Claude Rawson (1973) captures the extreme fluidity of Swift's satire in a way which overcomes 'the rigidities of mask-criticism' and conveys in a sensitive way the powerful energies and impulses which are present in the work. What he provides is an account of what it is like to read Swift's satire as a medium which expresses, enacts and displays a complex set of opinions, prejudices and impulses – to read his satire, that is, as a subtle and complex combination of artistry and self-expression.

It is criticism of Rawson's kind, which seeks to capture the movement of Swift's satire rather than reducing it to a set of fixed positions, which seems most adequately to provide what is needed. It does not dispense entirely with notions of character, persona or mask but these are seen as subordinate elements within the total experience of reading.

Style and satirical method

Rhetorical criticism as commonly practised in the 1950s and 1960s was helpful in defining terms, in demonstrating generic relationships and in clarifying the nature of the constituent elements of literature. But in its preoccupation with literary typology it can often seem remote from the actual experience of reading and interpreting individual texts. 'Irony', a key word in the vocabulary of Swift critics, was for example the subject of a number of general studies but none of them throws as much light upon what is happening as one reads *Gulliver's Travels* as one might expect. The reason is not far to seek: Swift's ways of using language and his satirical method are so complex and fluid as to defy description except by a holistic method which observes the process in action.

For a long time rhetorical studies of Swift's writing were essentially studies of Swift's prose style. The first sustained treatment of his writings from this point of view is the lectures delivered by Hugh Blair as Professor of Rhetoric in the University of Edinburgh and published in 1783. Blair saw Swift as being the foremost exponent of 'the Plain Style' – a way of writing which while sometimes negligent 'maintains the easy natural manner of an unaffected speaker'. The passages he selects for analysis are not taken from *Gulliver's Travels* but his description of the 'humorous' writings is apt: 'The plainness of his manner gives his wit a singular edge, and sets it off to higher advantage. There is no froth, nor affectation in it; it flows without any studied preparation; and while he hardly appears to smile himself, he makes his reader laugh heartily' (Williams, 1970, p.212). Herbert Read's account in *English Prose Style* (1928) stresses the simplicity and comprehensibility of Swift's style and the absence of imagery apart from that contained in common speech.

Although several later accounts start from Swift's plain style (and in some cases link Gulliver's style with the Royal Society's encouragement of simple, lucid expression), it is really only when that style is related to the particular tasks it is required to perform that it can be seen as part of Swift's complete manner and method as a satirist. In his discussion of Swift (1934) F.R. Leavis sets *Gulliver's Travels* to one side as if it were untypical of Swift's writing, preferring to concentrate instead upon *A Tale of a Tub* and *A Modest Proposal*. But since the development of critical awareness of those two works has had an important influence upon modern views of Swift's artistry, it is not surprising that Leavis provided a number of influential pointers. He registers the mental and emotional qualities which Swift's writing displays (energy, 'an extraordinary play of mind', self-assertion) but as these manifest themselves through the text they all have rhetorical significance. Leavis notes, for example, the way in which evenness of tone goes hand in hand with surprise: 'Surprise is a perpetually varied accompaniment of the grave, dispassionate, matter-of-fact tone in which Swift delivers his intensities'. And, here contrasting Swift and Gibbon, he suggests that Swift creates an impression of 'implied solidarity' with the reader which is then used as 'a means of betrayal'.

G. Wilson Knight's essay (1939) includes an apt description of the deceptiveness of Swift's calm, controlled manner. Swift does not, he says, 'give any impression of actual savagery' but 'writes as though well above his subject, with a deadly ease and serenity of statement'. He shows also that through 'the technique of leaving things out, the use of suggestion', Swift relies upon the reader's ability 'to do the rest' by producing the required thought from his own mind. And he suggests with particular reference to *Gulliver's Travels* that the key lies in the initial choice of a sym- bolic, sensory-physical structure: 'Swift's famous understatement and lucidity depend mainly on his first finding satirical-symbolic scenes so exactly suited that barest narration releases all the emotional force desired'. Wilson Knight is a sensitive reader of Swift, alive to the smallest effects, as when he notes how Gulliver's exhibition of nautical skill in sailing his little boat is put into perspective when Glumdalclitch hangs the boat on a nail to dry. Martin Price in *Swift's Rhetorical Art* (1953) develops Wilson Knight's point in his discussion of what he calls the 'symbolic works'. He sees the creation of reductive symbolic patterns as Swift's distinctive method and stresses that 'a middle view is left for the reader to define', a remark which relates clearly but not exclusively to the dialectical structure of the fourth voyage.

In his helpful introduction to Swift's satirical method D. W. Jefferson dissents from the received view that the key to Swift's art lies in the simplicity of his prose style. He finds it instead in what Swift shares with Rabelais, Donne and Ben Jonson – his skill, as an exponent of learned wit, in the dialectical manipulation of ideas. This is an obvious feature of Swift's earliest extended satire, *A Tale of a Tub*, but it is in evidence also in *Gulliver's Travels* behind the assumed manner of a plain man telling a plain tale. In keeping with this tradition of learned play, the Houyhnhnms are 'a device', 'an idea to be played with, offer- ing scope for the indulgence of temperamental animus, but not be taken too seriously'. 'There is', says Jefferson, 'an outrageous thesis to be proved, an ingenious exploitation of logic for that purpose and a translation of the ideas into concrete conceptions ("arguing through images"); and in the development of the concrete elements there is a significant ordering of detail to produce a tendentious distortion of the truth' (Jefferson, 1957, p.249).

A. E. Dyson (1958, *Casebook*), Herbert Davis and Hugh Sykes Davies (both Vickers, 1968) all return to the ostensible subject of Leavis's essay, Swift's irony. For Dyson, who has much of value to say about the traps Swift sets for the reader in presenting the Houyhnhnms, irony ceases for Swift to be 'a functional technique' and becomes 'the embodiment of an attitude to life'. For Sykes Davies irony is the method by which the eighteenth century achieved what the Elizabethans achieved more directly and one in which the reader is made an active partner in working out the message. One illuminating instance from Herbert Davis's essay, in which he distils some of his long acquaintance with Swift as editor of the standard edition of the prose writings, may serve as a reminder that the plainness of Swift's prose and its avoidance of metaphor does not exclude powerful resonances. Having returned from his final voyage, Gulliver speaks of his reception by his family and confesses: 'To this hour they dare not presume to touch my bread, or drink out of the same cup'. The bread and the cup, together with the word 'presume', call to mind the Anglican communion service ('We do not presume to come to this table'). Thus, Davis suggests, the breaking of a simple domestic bond carries sacramental overtones which heighten our sense of the abnormality of Gulliver's estrangement, his excommunication, from his own kind.

The references in Leavis's, Dyson's and Sykes Davies' accounts to the betrayal, entrapment or involvement of the reader are all of particular significance, for they contribute to the modern recognition that one of the essential elements of an encounter with Swift is the unsettling relationship which he establishes with his readers. C. J. Rawson, *Gulliver and the Gentle Reader*, explains this in terms of a prevailing sense of uncertainty as to how we should 'take' what Swift says. He notes the 'curious precariousness of the reader's grasp of what is going on' and speaks of 'continuous defensive uneasiness' and 'an undermining of our nervous poise', and in doing so catches something of the quicksilver quality of Swift's satire (Rawson, 1973).

Historical and contextual approaches

'The peruser of Swift wants little previous knowledge; it will be sufficient that he is acquainted with common words and common things'. Although *Gulliver's Travels* remains accessible to the general reader, much of what was common knowledge to Dr Johnson when he wrote these words in 1781 can now only be recovered through historical study, and few critics would disagree with Louis I. Bredvold's assertion that Swift's satire 'can be fully understood only as part of the history of his time' (Clifford, 1959, p.7).

It may be difficult to establish in theoretical terms what this actually means, for we can neither escape our own modern consciousness nor assume that of an eighteenth-century reader. But since, like most satirical writing, *Gulliver's Travels* stands in close relationship to the age and society which gave it birth we require knowledge of that context. For Gulliver, as for the reader, his journeys are not an escape from the known world so much as a new encounter with it; wherever the landfall, it is the England and Europe of his age that he discovers there. Swift could see the universal through the topicalities of his own place and time but his starting point was the world around him and without some knowledge of that world we may be blind to some of the things he reveals.

It is probably true to say that almost all of those who have written about *Gulliver's Travels* have felt the need at some point or other to relate the book to its contemporary context, and the whole approach of some is suffused with historical considerations. Thus the targets of the book's satire, the world-view it embodies, its meaning, its sources, Gulliver's outlook and role, even the book's style and form, have all been explained by reference to the ideas, writings and circumstances of Swift's own age.

Source studies

Although Swift gave *Gulliver'sTravels* the appearance of a plainly rendered account of first-hand experience, it is generally accepted that in writing it he drew deeply upon a lifetime's wide and various reading. In its way the *Travels* is no less bookish than *A Tale of a Tub*, Swift's other book-length satire, but here there is little overt evidence of the earlier mock-learned play with references to scholarly authorities, to Pausanias, Herodotus, Lucretius, Ctesias, Wotton, Bentley and a host of other ancient and modern authors. The echoes and evidences of Swift's reading are now deeply embedded in a narrative manner which deliberately eschews learned ostentation. But concealed though they may be, the parallels discovered between the *Travels* and other texts are so numerous and so important to an understanding of the book that the results of source study represent one of the essential foundations for interpretation and commentary.

Although earlier criticism contains many scattered references to writings which may have influenced Swift, the first full and systematic survey of the sources of *Gulliver's Travels* was undertaken by the American scholar William A. Eddy whose *Gulliver's Travels: A Critical Study* (1923) remains a standard reference work on the subject. Eddy's primary concern is with *Gulliver's Travels* as a 'philosophic voyage' and he shows that Swift was working in an already well-established tradition. In writing the voyage to Lilliput, for example, he would have been able to draw upon a substantial literature describing mythical pygmy commonwealths. In creating Brobdingnag he may well have recalled incidents from Cyrano de Bergerac's *Comic History of the Moon* (1656) where, in a land of giants, Cyrano is made to perform as a dwarf in a circus, is taken to court and becomes the pet of the queen and courtiers, and proves to be the subject of disagreement among the philosophers who are asked to determine his species. The same book provides a source for the fourth voyage – a sweeping condemnation of human nature pronounced by a tribunal of animals in which it is made clear that 'man, not his fellow creatures, is the real brute'. One effect of Eddy's findings is to accentuate the traditional character of Swift's satirical strategies. Although Eddy shared his generation's distaste for the Voyage to the Houyhnhnms, he shows that unfavourable contrasts between degenerate European civilisations (represented by the traveller) and ideal human commonwealths or superior races of animals are standard features of utopian fictions before Swift and therefore not necessarily indicative of exceptional misanthropy.

A steady stream of books and learned articles has over the years identified many additional sources. Some of the most notable take the discussion into areas neglected by Eddy.

These include the contributions of Marjorie Nicolson (Swift and contemporary science), R. W. Frantz (Gulliver and contemporary voyages of discovery), R. S. Crane (the fourth voyage and scholastic logic), and others noted in the following pages.

History of ideas

> These persons upon their return began to dislike the management of everything below, and fell into schemes of putting all arts, sciences, languages and mechanics upon a new foot. ... But as for himself, being not of an enterprising spirit, he was content to go on in the old forms, to live in the houses his ancestors had built, and act as they did in every part of life without innovation. (*GT* 221–2)

Leslie Stephen said that no author 'can free himself from the habits of thought of his time' and in this sense all literature belongs to the history of ideas. But there are works which so strongly embody and so directly address issues of a specifically philosophical or ideological character as to demand from the reader some prior knowledge of the intellectual climate from which they issue. *Gulliver's Travels* is a book of this kind. In its general conception, in the characterisation of Gulliver and in innumerable significant details it reveals itself as a reaction to the religious, intellectual and scientific tendencies of its age and for many critics it can only be properly explained and interpreted in that light.

The passage quoted above follows Gulliver's description of Munodi's estate which in its orderliness and fertility is contrasted with the disruption wrought by unregulated innovation. The satire is specifically directed at the Royal Society or the contemporary craze for 'projects' and speculative schemes, but the passage expresses in microcosm a more general sense of disdain for modernising change and of regret at the passing of well-tried, traditional ways. Swift himself was pre-eminently one of those content 'to go on in the old forms' and, in an age making decisive shifts in ideas and social organisation towards a 'modern' consciousness and social order, this inevitably left him, as he was latterly in politics, in opposition to and alienation from major currents of change. Many of the most significant modern contributions to Swift criticism adopt a history of ideas approach, drawing upon the resources of what has become through the labours of scholars such as A.O. Lovejoy, Marjorie Nicolson and R.S. Crane an academic specialism in its own right. The first service of this kind of scholarship is to set the scene by providing a general account of the intellectual movements which enables us to make sense of Swift's attitude.

What the historians of ideas show of the eighteenth century is a polarisation of attitudes of the kind reflected in the above quotation, with Swift on the side of orthodoxy and traditionalism. Optimism and benevolence are ranged against pessimistic views of human nature, the advocacy of the new science against the defence of older forms of humanistic learning, speculative philosophy against practical common sense, rationalism in religion against a traditional dependence upon divine revelation, in short the modern against the traditional. Leslie Stephen laid the groundwork for later scholars in his monumental *History of English Thought in the Eighteenth Century* (1896) where, while acknowledging their differences, he couples Swift and Johnson as the two most vigorous representatives of a world-view which shows little regard for the voluminous theorising of the philosophers and theologians who are Stephen's main subject:

> Their eyes are fixed upon the world around them, and they regard as foolish and presumptuous any one who dares to contemplate the great darkness. The expression of this sentiment in literature is a marked disposition to turn aside from pure speculation, combined with a deep interest in social and moral laws. ... We know not what we are, nor whither we are going, nor whence we came; but we can, by the help of common sense, discover a sufficient share of moral maxims for our guidance in life, and we can analyse human passions, and discover what are the moving forces of society, without going back to first principles. (1962 reprint, II, p.315)

Valuable, more recent, accounts include Louis I. Bredvold's 'The Gloom of the Tory Satirists' (1949, reprinted in Clifford, 1959) and Paul Fussell's *The Rhetorical World of Augustan Humanism* (1965). Using the word to imply an outlook nurtured by the values and culture which derives from classical Graeco-Roman civilisation, Fussell nominates as 'humanists' writers such as Swift, Pope and Johnson. He defines their outlook in a list of distinctive attitudes. They doubt the probability of progress, believe that most human problems cannot be solved, feel veneration for the past, believe that man's primary obligation is to address himself to moral questions and not scientific ones, are convinced that human nature is irremediably flawed, are suspicious of simplifying theories of government or human nature, believe that the value of literature and art is primarily moral, and believe in the uniqueness of man as a species. Accounts such as Stephen's and Fussell's may in their generality seem remote from our text, but it is attitudes such as those they elicit which help to explain the direction of, for example, the third voyage and the approval given to the values and priorities of the Brobdingnagians who, in their preoccupation with useful and applied knowledge, have no conception of 'ideas, entities, abstractions and transcendentals' (*GT* 176). They are, in Fussell's sense, humanists.

Fundamental to the Swiftian world-view is his attitude to human nature and this provides the focus for T.O. Wedel's important essay 'On the Philosophical Background of *Gulliver's Travels*' (1926, *Casebook*, pp.83–99). For Wedel the *Travels* embodies a world view which was out of tune with the growing contemporary emphasis upon man's benevolent instincts and capacity for goodness – and he shows that much of the hostile contemporary criticism was written from this standpoint. Had the book been published a few generations earlier, he suggests, it would not have seemed unusually misanthropic, for Swift's emphasis upon the corruption of human nature and the limitations of human reason was until the eighteenth century a standard feature of Christian moralising. However:

> By the year 1726, in England at least, the restitution of human nature was already well underway. The dignity of human nature was already on everyone's lips. Locke and the Deists had given man a new trust in Reason; the Cambridge Platonists and Shaftesbury were discovering in him a moral sense, even in the hitherto despised realm of the passions. Nothing seems more certain to the new age than the existence of a beneficent deity, and the consequent goodness of his creation. Optimistic theodicies are being written on all sides, explaining away the evil from this best of all possible worlds.

The contrasting view of human nature presented in *Gulliver's Travels* coincides, for example, with that of Bayle who regards Man as an ungovernable animal given over to evil whose reason is all too easily overcome by his passions and who, in view of all these deficiencies, can rely only on divine grace.

Wedel's general account of conflicting views of human nature is the prelude to an analysis of the fourth voyage in which he makes a number of important contributions to the unfolding debate about this most contentious section of the book. He identifies as of key importance Swift's letter to Pope dated

29 September 1725 in which, alluding to *Gulliver's Travels*, then in progress, he speaks of his detestation of 'that animal called man' and his love for individuals and goes on:

> I have got materials toward a treatise proving the falsity of that definition *animal rationale*, and to show it should be only *rationis capax*. Upon this great foundation of misanthropy (though not in Timon's manner) the whole building of my Travels is erected; and I never will have peace of mind till all honest men are of my opinion.

This has been the cornerstone of many subsequent interpretations of the fourth voyage. Wedel also advances a view of the dialectical structure of the final voyage which relates the Houyhnhnms and the Yahoos with two conflicting world-views. Recalling Thomas Hobbes's well-known description of the life of Man in a state of nature as 'solitary, poor, nasty, brutish, and short' and Locke's description of Man in the same state as 'living together according to reason, without a common superior', he suggests that we have in the miserable primitivism of the Yahoos Hobbe's view contrasted with Locke's rational and egalitarian commonwealth. As for Gulliver, he occupies a position midway between the two, 'part beast, part reason'. He is not, like the Houyhnhmns, wholly rational, nor yet devoid of reason like the Yahoos. He is instead capable of reason (as Swift puts it in his letter, *rationis capax*). What seems a very acceptable interpretation has already taken form.

Subsequent critics offer various amplifications and refinements. Roland M. Frye (1954), for example, emphasises the specifically Christian antecedents of Swift's satire when he shows that the Yahoos are conceived in a tradition which uses images of the human body, its functions and physical corruptions in representing human depravity. He cites many passages from the Bible and the sermons and writings of Christian divines of which the following may give some impression of their combined denunciatory force: 'What is man but a vessel of dung, a stink of corruption, and, by birth, a slave of the devil?' 'Without this body man had been an Angel; and without this soul but a Brute.' 'What a charnel-house of stinking carrion is this body and life of wicked man.' Another important dimension is added by R. W. Frantz (1931) who shows that the accounts of the voyagers (many of which Swift is known to have read) are full of descriptions of encounters with primitive races and simians which are almost invariably presented as loathsome real-life examples of Man in an unregenerate condition. There is little doubt that the Yahoos are based upon them.

The role of the Yahoos has proved to be more straightforward to explain than that of the Houyhnhnms. For a long time the horses of the last voyage were assumed to represent Swift's (and not merely Gulliver's) ideal state and since they appeared repellent in their lack of so much that enriches human existence this inevitably raised questions about the adequacy of Swift's positives and indeed of his hold on reality. (On this see Leavis and Orwell.) However, the assumption that they are exempt from Swiftian humour came to be questioned by critics who saw something intentionally comic in the solemnly-conducted daily routines of these humourless creatures who, for all their much-vaunted perfection, are peculiarly ill-suited to such ordinary tasks as building a house or threading a needle. (See the articles by John F. Ross, 1941, and W.E. Yeomans, 1966, reprinted in Gravil, 1974.) In that it identified the Houyhnhnms with a specific philosophical position liable to be ridiculed by Swift, Wedel's suggestion that they represent a Lockean view of life in a state of nature foreshadowed other 'philosophical' interpretations of the Houyhnhnms. Kathleen Williams and Irvin Ehrenpreis both argued that far from embodying Swift's conception of the ideal life the horses represent the inadequacy and negativity of a life of pure rationality, and thus in turn the deficiencies of a Deistic or Stoic world-view. Williams presented a first version of this view in an article published in 1951 (*Casebook*, pp.136–47) and a more elaborate account in her major study *Jonathan Swift and the Age of Compromise* (1958). Here she establishes a specific link between Deism and the Houyhnhnms through the anti-Christian Utopian voyages written by French *libertins*. She instances Gabriel de Foigny's *La Terre Australe Connue* (1676, English translation 1693), a source noted by Eddy, in which a race of hermaphrodites exhibit many of the characteristics of the Houyhnhnms. They are governed by reason, eat no flesh, have all things in common, go naked (like Adam and Eve before the Fall), and live in unbroken amity without the necessity for governmental authority. Ehrenpreis's general thesis is similar, although the specifics are quite different. He notes that the words of Gulliver's Houyhnhnm master ('*Reason* alone is sufficient to govern a *rational* creature') are 'contrary to the spirit of Christianity' and represent a position Swift explicitly condemned in his sermons on the Conscience and the Excellency of Christianity. He cites parallels from notable Deists detested by Swift ('To be governed by reason is the general law imposed by the author of nature') and then claims that Swift was aiming at one 'particular exponent of deistic thought', Swift's friend, Viscount Bolingbroke, with whom he argued by letter about religion (Ehrenpreis, 1958, chapter 5).

When these new views of the Houyhnhnms first appeared in the 1950s several prominent Swiftians were quick to dissent. Ehrenpreis's identification of Bolingbroke provoked disagreement but even the more general point that the rationalism of the Houyhnhnms is incompatible with Christian theology was not accepted. By the time he wrote his important article 'The Meaning of Gulliver's Last Voyage' Ehrenpreis's thinking had moved on, so much so that he acknowledged a debt to George Sherburn's and Louis Landa's critical comments on his earlier essay. A more important influence on Ehrenpreis was that of R. S. Crane who made a discovery which might stand as a model of the way in which the study of sources can illuminate meaning. Crane prefaces his discovery with an exposition of principles for the use of evidence drawn from the history of ideas (principles which Ehrenpreis and Williams had not observed), but when he delivers his own argument it is so neat and so convincing that it is like the last piece of a jigsaw dropping into place.

One essential clue is in Swift's letter of 1725 quoted by Wedel: the definition *animal rationale* which, it is clear with hindsight, has connotations of formal logic. Another is the logical structure of the fourth voyage itself with its three terms — horses, yahoo, and man. Crane shows that there is a remarkable correspondence between this three-part structure and the examples used in the formal syllogistic logic which in Swift's day was part of the curriculum at Trinity College, Dublin, and other universities. The logical exercises practised by the undergraduates typically involved the classification of various creatures and things according to their distinguishing characteristics and points of difference (*differentia*). The commonest of all the several examples taken for illustration and practice is the proposition that man is a rational animal. Crane quotes a passage from a Dutch logician, Francis Burgersdyck, as an example of a series of logical distinctions leading to this very conclusion.

It states that Man and Angel are substances, distinguished by the fact that Man is corporeal and Angel not. Man and Stone are both corporeal substances but Man is animate and Stone inanimate. Man and Plant are animate corporeal substances but Man has feeling and Plant is void of feeling. Finally, Man and Horse are both animate corporeal feeling substances but Man is rational and Horse irrational. Thus, Crane shows, the framework is ready-made for a disorientating satirical reversal by the invention of 'a world in which horses appeared where the logicians had put men and men where they had put horses'.

One of the several attractions of Crane's interpretation is that it makes sense of the logical structure of the last voyage as an integrated unit and does not leave any one part of the pattern to carry the meaning. So well does it fit the facts of the case that it now takes priority over 'deistic' explanations of the Houyhnhnms, although these have not been wholly discarded. (Martin Kallich in his study of religious elements in *Gulliver's Travels* (1970, p.74) entertains the view that, 'unenriched by a revealed faith, which to Swift is absolutely fundamental to the truly religious life, the horses can . . . aptly become the objects of his satire'.) Crane's interpretation was, as noted above, adopted by Ehrenpreis as part of a further reading of 'The Meaning of Gulliver's Last Voyage' (Ehrenpreis, 1962) which supplements it in several valuable ways. He draws attention to the fact that the logicians make play not merely with 'man' and 'horse' but also with 'ape' thus extending the logical pattern to include the ape-like Yahoos. And, in relation to this, he shows that in the *Essay on Human Understanding* (1690) and in his dispute with Bishop Stillingfleet John Locke confronts the problem of finding a comprehensive definition of man which takes sufficient account of such unsettling examples as apes which 'have shapes like ours, but are hairy, and want language and reason', idiots 'that have perfectly our shape, but want reason, and some of them language too' and of Peter who after a blow to the head at the age of thirty has 'not so much appearance of reason in him, as in his horse or monkey'. Ehrenpreis's reading gains from the combination of historical contextualisation with a keen sense of the elusive way in which Swift's satire operates, which makes it perilous to read the last voyage as a rigidly consistent allegory. Thus he gives due weight to the admirable characters – the King of Brobdingnag, Lord

Munodi, Captain Pedro de Mendez – who offer an alternative, humanly attainable ideal and to the element of humour with which the Houyhnhnms are presented. This humour perhaps warns 'the sophisticated reader that this author, unlike Gulliver, appreciates the comical aspects of his own didacticism'.

The debate goes on. Carefully documenting many parallels between the two, Ian Higgins has recently demonstrated that Houyhnhnm society closely resembles the austere civilisation of ancient Sparta. Admired by Swift and some of his contemporaries, the Spartans were condemned by Bernard Mandeville for a quality of life which later critics found repellent in the Houyhnhnms: 'the only thing they could be proud of, was, that they enjoy'd nothing'. The effect of Higgins's analysis is to renew the idea that the Houyhnhnms are a positive: 'Swift set out to vex his readers by creating a rational Spartan order that he intended to be admired but that was shown to be unattainable for modern man' (Higgins, 1983, p.530).

The history of science

We have dealt so far with aspects of eighteenth-century philosophical and theological thought which relate to Swift's view of human nature. Another branch of the history of ideals which has relevance to *Gulliver's Travels* deals specifically with the development of scientific ideas. This relates most obviously to the satire of science in the third voyage but it also provides a necessary element of the general intellectual context of the *Travels*. Swift lived in an age which was digesting the scientific revolution of the seventeenth century. At a superficial level, this issued in a multiplicity of curious and seemingly trivial enquiries (as ridiculed in the Voyage to Laputa) but, more fundamentally, it was transforming the way in which mankind perceived the universe and apprehended reality. Traditional wisdom and divine revelation were no longer seen as adequate guides to truth; the new thinkers and experimental scientists insisted instead 'that the world is utterly rational, composed of nothing but matter and motion, and that only rational, anti-mystical methods of thought could therefore comprehend it' (M. B Hall (ed.), *Nature and Nature's Laws*, 1970, p.7). Tradition and authority were being dethroned by empiricism and part of Swift's life-work was to help fight a rearguard action against that change and all it implied. (The disparaging allusions to Descartes, Gassendi and Newton (unnamed) in Chapter VIII of Voyage III are indicative of his attitude.)

A key work for the understanding of Swift's satire of science is Marjorie Nicolson's and Nora Mohler's study 'The Scientific Background of Swift's "Voyage to Laputa"' (1935, reprinted Jeffares, 1967) which identifies many parallels between the *Travels* and contemporary scientific literature. Their principal source is the *Philosophical Transactions of the Royal Society*, the Society's official record of meetings, papers and experiments, and this bears witness to the extremely diverse and often curious lines of enquiry being pursued by men of learning. Swift could there have found, alongside the contributions of Newton, Halley, Wren and Hooke, accounts of long-lived Bramines who bear a resemblance to the Struldbruggs, and papers on such Laputan preoccupations as comets and the mathematical interpretation of music, together with records of experiments which anticipate even the most bizarre projects undertaken by members of the Academy of Lagado. Notes on a blind man's sensitivity to colour, experiments with air pumps, dogs, spider's silk, plant respiration and sunbeams, and new methods of agriculture amply warrant the conclusion that 'for the most part [Swift] simply set down before his readers experiments actually performed by members of the Royal Society', occasionally combining or taking real experiments one step further until we are carried 'over the precipice of nonsense'. Extracts from scientific papers are included, with a commentary, in Clive T. Probyn's *Jonathan Swift: The Contemporary Background* (1978).

The value of researches of this kind goes beyond the identification of specific satirical sources. What also becomes clear is that in spite of Swift's evident antipathy to the 'new science' of the Royal Society, *Gulliver's Travels* is deeply imbued with its spirit and its way of looking at the world. Thus another of Marjorie Nicholson's important studies, 'The Microscope and English Imagination' (1935), is a reminder of how much the Voyages to Lilliput and Brobdingnag must owe to the microscope and astronomical telescope in opening to the mind the prospect of much smaller and larger worlds. Indeed, as she says, the *Travels* 'could not have been written before the period of the microscope'. Researches into seventeenth- and

eighteenth-century travel literature also enable us to relate
Lemuel Gulliver himself to the scientific movement. As R. W.
Frantz and W. H. Bonner show, the *Travels* is written in the
manner of William Dampier ('Cousin Dampier' in 'A Letter to
Sympson', p.37) and Gulliver himself is a traveller in the same
mould, that is to say not a mere adventurer but one who feels
himself obliged to respond to the Royal Society's requests to
voyagers to collect and record data on everything they witness:
'Let them . . . always have a Table-Book at hand to set down
everything worth remembring . . . the Climate, Government,
Power, Places'. There are unmistakable reminders of this in
Gulliver's actions (he weighs a hailstone and presents specimens
to Gresham's College, the headquarters of the Royal Society) and
in his style, which is plain and unadorned in the manner recom-
mended by the Society. Thomas Sprat commended the rejection
of 'amplifications, digressions, and swellings of style' and the
return to 'primitive purity, and shortness, when men deliver'd so
many *things*, almost in an equal number of *words*' (Probyn, 1978,
p.60). Given this interest in language, it is significant that Swift
introduced linguistic projects into Lagado, most notably in the
writing frame and the scheme to use *things* rather than *words*,
which echoes Sprat's dualistic view of language. As C. T. Probyn
shows ('Swift and Linguistics', *Neophilologus* 58, 1974), these
projects are a satirical reflection of the mechanistic schemes
of John Wilkins, one of the founders of the Royal Society.

The interconnections between the new science and contemporary views of language and human understanding are extremely
complex and a comprehensive account of their bearing upon
Gulliver's Travels has yet to be written. Increasingly, however,
critics have recognised their relevance and the book's 'epistemological' themes are now seen as being as significant as its moral
and political ones. Thus in *Lemuel Gulliver's Mirror for Man* (1968)
W. B. Carnochan advances the view that the book should be
regarded as a commentary on Locke's *Essay concerning Human
Understanding*, one of the seminal statements of the new outlook.
Interpretations of *A Tale of a Tub* as a satire on contemporary
ideas have contributed to this recognition (see M. K. Starkman,
Swift's Satire on Learning in A Tale of a Tub, 1950, reprinted 1968).
Two recent epistemological interpretations deal conjointly with
A Tale and the *Travels*: Frances D. Louis's *Swift's Anatomy of Mis-
understanding: A Study of Swift's Epistemological Imagination* (1981)

and Everett Zimmerman's *Swift's Narrative Satires* (1983). Dr Louis specifically depreciates traditional personal and political interpretations of the *Travels*: it is, she says, 'far more significantly and accurately the history of how men thought about themselves and about the nature of thinking itself' (p.xvii). Gulliver's way of looking at the world is central to this kind of interpretation as is clear from Hugh Kenner's lively discussion in *The Counterfeiters* (1968, reprinted Donoghue, 1971). Kenner invites his reader to compare Gulliver with a sophisticated computer. He may answer questions correctly but, such are the limitations of his awareness, his humanity remains in doubt. Gulliver, 'the complete empiricist . . . empiricism itself, trousered and shirted, . . . observes, observes, observes' but reveals 'utter ignorance of everything save navigation, a little applied mathematics, and medicine. Civilisation is a memory, . . . history, the classics, the works which we have learned to call humane letters . . . are as if unknown to him.' Yet, says Kenner, 'he is our representative', 'the carrier and incarnation of the values we really value'. Seen in this way, the limitations and fallibility of Gulliver's reactions, his omissions and misjudgements, are not merely the comic shortcomings of an individual but an integral part of Swift's satirical indictment of a world-view – a modern scientific world-view – which is fundamentally deficient.

Politics

> How could that which I spoke so many years ago, and at above five thousand leagues distance, in another reign, be applied to any of the Yahoos who now are said to govern the herd? (*GT* 37–8)

This is Gulliver's retrospective view of the attachment to the *Travels* of specific political meetings. The declaration of innocence may be no accurate guide to Swift's actual intentions but the view, long current, that the political significance of *Gulliver's Travels* rests upon a series of reflections upon actual individuals and events from then recent political history has of late been called into question. There is no reason to doubt the identification of the Lilliputian High Heels and Low Heels with, respectively, the High Church party (Tories) and the Low Church party (Whigs) or the interpretation of the Egg controversy as an allegorical account of the division between Roman Catholicism and Anglicanism from the time of Henry VIII. What has come to be questioned is the discovery of precise historical counter-parts for individuals and events in the Voyage to Lilliput.

Any account of the book's political aspects needs to take account of the earliest reactions to it. Bertrand Goldgar (*Walpole and the Wits*, 1976) provides an interesting account of its reception and of the circumstances in which political meanings were identified by the earliest commentators. He leaves open the question as to what extent it was Swift's intention that the book should be read as a thinly masked allegory of British political life but he shows that, first appearing as it did on the eve of a new wave of propaganda against Walpole and his government, it was absorbed into that campaign and provided powerful motifs for it. 'Whether Swift wished it or not, his book was received almost at once as a decidedly political document and was both understood and used as a contribution to the political journalism of the opposition' (p.50). The testimony of Swift's contemporaries may seem on the face of it to offer the most authentic guide to the meanings supposed to be implanted there, but their motives were not above suspicion. Whether out of a desire to make mischief for Swift or to recruit his satire to their cause, they may be unreliable explicators.

Nonetheless the early identifications were adopted and used as a model of the type of reading the book warranted. Sir Walter Scott said of Lilliput that 'the great scope and tendency of the satire is here levelled against the court and ministry of George I. . . . the tone of the satire . . . strictly personal'. In this reading Flimnap is Walpole and Gulliver's flight to Blefuscu an allusion to Bolingbroke and Atterbury who, accused of high treason, had taken refuge in France. Such interpretations remained current through the nineteenth century, although it is worth noting that Henry Craik saw the political allusions as occasional 'side strokes' and 'not systematic' (Craik, 1894, II, p.121). In 1919 the historian Sir Charles Firth codified and amplified them in a paper which for many years seemed to be the last word on the subject. Many of the identifications were the received ones (Flimnap as Walpole, the Emperor as George I, the hobbling Prince as the Prince of Wales). Certain additions have come to seem much more questionable: Galbet, the morose and sour High Admiral as the Earl of Nottingham (nicknamed 'Dismal'), the Emperor's cushion (which saved Flimnap from a fall) as

George I's mistress, and the ill-received extinction of the fire by urine as Swift's similarly well-intentioned and ill-received *A Tale of a Tub*. Firth's reliance upon a theory that the text of the first voyage is made up of layers composed in 1714 and layers composed some ten years later no longer wholly accords with what is known about the composition of the book.

In its comprehensiveness and its specificity, if not in the acceptability of some of its judgements, A. E. Case's chapter on 'Personal and Political Satire in *Gulliver's Travels*' (Case, 1945 reprinted 1958) overtakes Firth. High Heels and Low Heels, Bigendians and Little Endians, George I and the Prince of Wales, Nottingham and Flimnap figure in Case's interpretation with much the same identifications as Firth's but according to a different scheme. Whereas Firth saw the first voyage as textually and satirically an amalgam of passages relating to Queen Anne's reign (1702–14) and George I's (1714–27), Case argues that Gulliver's Lilliputian adventures represent the joint political fortunes of Oxford and Bolingbroke in the latter half of Queen Anne's reign when they were joint leaders of the Tory government, while the third voyage focuses on the Whig ministry in George I's reign. Apart from his insistence upon allegorical and chronological consistency, Case's interpretation is notable for ingenuity in dealing with small particulars. Not every account finds a place for Flimnap's informers Clustril and Drunlo, but in Case's reading they are Walpole's spies Pancier and Neynoe. His explanation of Gulliver's dousing of the palace fire is also ingenious: it represents the Tories' illegal negotiation of a peace, and the unseemliness of his action corresponds with Oxford's drunkenness and offensive language in the presence of Queen Anne. 'Gulliver saved the palace, though his conduct was both illegal and indecent: Oxford saved the state, in return for which incidental illegalities and indecencies should be overlooked'.

Case's tendency to particularise the satire is seen also in his treatment of the Flying Island in the third voyage. Most commentators would agree that in a general way it is an allegorical representation of England's economic and political disadvantaging of Ireland. But Case goes further. He sees the 'Tall rocks', 'high Spires' and pillars of stone which could damage the adamantine bottom of the island as the threat posed in a constitutional collision by, respectively, the nobility, the church and the citizenry. In a similar way he gives all

the details of the revolt of Lindalino (III, chap. 3) topical
significance: the strong pointed rock is the Irish Church
or St Patrick's Cathedral, the four towers equate with the
Privy Council, the Grand Jury and the two houses of the
Irish Parliament, and the combustible fuel with the incendiary
pamphlets written against Wood's halfpence by Swift and others.

The interpretations of Firth and Case held sway for a long
time. But in 1969 W. A. Speck argued that there is deliberate ambi-
guity about the actual historical counterparts of the Lilliputian
politicians. 'They could all belong to William's reign, or to
Anne's, or to George I's', they could be interpreted differently by
Whigs and Tories, and Flimnap could just as well be Godolphin
in Queen Anne's reign as Walpole in George I's. The result was
to reveal a much less partisan view of political history than
previous commentators had envisaged. In 1977 Case's readings
were challenged by J. A. Downie on grounds not only of over-
specificity and inflexible consistency but also of historical inac-
curacy. He returns, for example, to the palace fire to point out
that since Queen Anne approved the peace negotiations, which
were generally popular, she could hardly in allegory be seen as
hostile to them. Although Downie questions the soundness of
Case's method, he is willing to venture some readings of his
own. Bolgolam now becomes the military leader Marlborough
and, less probably, Munodi's mill (III, chap.4), because of the
association of 'mill' with coinage, alludes to Wood's halfpence.
Downie's vigorous criticisms are a reminder that we are dealing
with interpretations and not hard facts, and perhaps with an
assortment of allusions rather than a tightly logical allegory, but
what is most significant is that he shows a willingness to identify
the most important political aspects of *Gulliver's Travels* as being
in the second voyage – in Gulliver's conversations with the King
touching on the nature of good government – rather than in the
decipherment of an allegory. He concludes on this note: 'I would
like to see *Gulliver's Travels* emancipated from arguments over
political content, for the sake of the wider social satire. . . . It is
the timeless quality of social, not political, satire that makes the
work relevant to the modern reader'. Taken to its logical conclusion this argument assumes that Bolgolam, Reldresal, Munodi,
even Flimnap, become types, symbols, not actual personalities.

In his book, *The Politics of 'Gulliver's Travels'* (1980), F. P. Lock
also emphasises the generality of the book's political meaning

and is emphatic in criticising the scholarly ingenuity 'devoted to a wild-goose chase after interpretations . . . that are more particular, topical, and personal than the nature of the satire warrants' (p.89). He does not deny that Swift introduced a number of particular references but he sees these as departures from Swift's original and over-riding plan to present 'a general satirical commentary on the follies of civilised man'. 'Swift's satire,' he says, 'could be applied to the contemporary scene, and he intended it to be; but it has no particular meaning limited to or determined by that scene' (p.90). Swift's method is, in short, to create types and paradigms based upon his knowledge of individuals. Thus even the most secure of the individual equations is questionable: Flimnap is first and foremost a typical royal favourite or prime minister rather than a representation of of Walpole.

Lock provides a valuable corrective to the particularity of previous interpretations, but he makes an even more important contribution in establishing the general vision of political history which informs the *Travels* as a whole. In terms of party allegiances Swift was Tory or 'old Whig' and his specific beliefs included those set out in his letter to Alexander Pope dated 10 January 1721, where he speaks of his support of the Protestant Succession and the Revolution Settlement, of his belief in annual parliaments, of the importance of landed possessions rather than money as the proper basis of political power, and of his own 'mortal antipathy against standing armies'. Implied in these beliefs is his clear preference for constitutional monarchy, a system in which power is subject to checks and balances and not exercised without regulation as in an absolutist state. In its pessimistic assumptions and nostalgic leanings his political outlook can, at a more general level, be seen as consistent with the general world-view described by Stephen, Bredvold and Fussell. It assumes the degeneracy and decline of modern England like the earlier decline of Sparta and Rome: the good society, of which in retrospect the reign of Queen Anne was a short-lived example, is located in the past. It emphasises also the role of the individual in politics; but in what Lock calls Swift's 'Cato complex' the only political heroes are seen to be those who, in worldly terms, are failures but who preserve their integrity in retirement or defeat. It is significant that a sextumvirate of men of this kind are singled out for special praise in Laputa (p.241) and that the admirable Lord Munodi has the air of an eminently sane man shunning and shunned by the fools and knaves currently in power. This is a reminder of what Lock underlines – that Swift's vision of political history is one which derives from his own study of history and is validated by the example of men he revered and by what he himself witnessed and experienced of political life.

It is clear that the debate about the political content of the *Travels* has not concluded. Downie, for example, feels that Lock takes the denial of specific contemporary references too far: 'The satire was indeed wide-ranging; it has a timeless quality, to be sure. But it was also, at times, stridently contemporary, and dangerously specific' (*British Journal for Eighteenth Century Studies*, Spring 1984).

Social history

The first voyage begins by firmly assigning Gulliver to his place in the social order, but by comparison with political history and the history of ideas, social history has been relatively neglected in discussions of *Gulliver's Travels*. A few notable contributions indicate that this is now changing.

Angus Ross's essay 'The Social Circumstances of Several Remote Nations of the World' (Vickers, 1968) points the way by showing that the text is at many points informed by the kinds of observation and social classification which reflect a society which was 'markedly and rigidly hierarchical'. He observes that in each of the voyages we are provided with carefully selected social details of the many individuals, institutions and customs Swift sets before us, not simply to lend the story authenticity but also out of a sense that society itself is 'a controlling force on human nature, *and* a corrupter of that nature'. Looked at sociologically Gulliver is seen to enter Lilliput 'from the top down' whereas the reverse is true of the second voyage. The famous and telling passage approving the growth of two ears of corn where only one grew before (*GT* 176), can be recognised as issuing naturally from the social circumstances of a nation 'where socio-economic doctrines are really important, not the *roman-à-clef* aspect which Firth tends to identify with the political importance of the book'.

Historical knowledge is valuable to criticism when it endows with significance what might otherwise be passed over. Aline M. Taylor's fascinating essay 'Sights and Monsters and Gulliver's

Voyage to Brobdingnag' (1957) is of this kind. She shows that Gulliver, as exhibited by the farmer in the early chapters of the second voyage and as subsequently petted by the Queen, is the precise counterpart of the midgets, monkeys, puppets and freaks who were displayed for popular entertainment in the eighteenth century. The circumstances in which the farmer exhibits Gulliver recall the practices of contemporary showmen, while his tricks and displays of skill are of exactly the kind which appeared in their handbills and advertisements. The box in which Gulliver lives and is transported and which is both pro- tection and prison was, above all, a familiar piece of apparatus while the ultimate indignity which Gulliver fears of being found a mate to bear his offspring was actually realised in the Little Family exhibited in London in 1712: a man three feet tall, his wife big with child and their little horse 'to be seen over against the Muse-Gate at Charing Cross'. Aline Taylor goes on to use her discoveries as a way of illustrating a complex web of motifs (animal, infant, toy and gladiator) and themes (relativity, impris- onment and pride) which lie at the heart of the second voyage in a way which gives significance to the seemingly incidental.

No present-day critic brings to bear upon Swift a more intimate or comprehensive knowledge of his social setting than Pat Rogers. His essay 'Gulliver's Glasses' (Probyn, 1978) starts with the witty insight that Gulliver is 'perhaps the first bespectacled hero in English literature' and proceeds by an interesting combination of close reading ('the word *observe* and its derivatives occur some 140 times in the work') and out-of-the-way knowledge of eighteenth-century ophthalmics to show that in a book in which the narrative is controlled through sense impressions, sight is the dominant means of apprehending reality. It is, moreover (and here Gulliver shares his author's own ambivalence) the faculty that permits close scrutiny of blemished breasts and lice-ridden beggars while allowing the observer to remain at a safe distance from the physical world. In another essay, 'Gulliver and the Engineers' (1975) Rogers reacts against the emphasis historians of ideas have placed upon the experimental and speculative science of the Royal Society as the context for *Gulliver's Travels*. The connotations of 'South Sea' (all of Gulliver's voyages take him to the southern hemisphere) and 'projector' point instead to the 'bustling, uncerebral world of entrepreneurs and inventors'. (The South Sea Company was a scandalous example of speculative investment.) This, Rogers argues, has relevance not only to Lagado; it even provides a context for the palace fire in Lilliput, for fire-fighting was a problem which had prompted many ingenious inventions.

'Landscape', a term so relevant in the study of Pope, seems almost alien to Swift. But in her recent study, *Swift's Landscape* (1982), Carole Fabricant shows how the actual features of Swift's world and his distinctive perception of them combine to constitute his personal landscape or 'country of the mind'. She deals with the well-worn topic of Swift's excremental vision by showing with detailed reference to conditions in the immediate vicinity of Swift's cathedral that he actually lived in a landscape in which excrement was a prominent, visible and necessarily obtrusive feature. In the same way, what Gulliver recoils from in Brobdingnag – maggots, lice and fleas – were features not merely of his satiric vision but of his 'geographic and sociological landscape'. And, taking up an earlier observation by Sir Charles Firth, she relates the Yahoos to the common people of Ireland on two counts – their reported slovenliness, squalor, barbarity and submissiveness to authority, together with their position as a servant class to a ruling elite. If this is so then the Houyhnhnms might be equated with the English ruling class in Ireland. All routes lead back, it seems, to the fourth voyage, and Swift's Irishness haunts the text in unpredictable ways.

PART TWO
APPRAISAL

Introduction: the world made strange

I proposed that Homer and Aristotle might appear at the head of all their commentators; but these were so numerous that some hundreds were forced to attend in the court and outward rooms of the palace. ... And I had a whisper from a ghost, who shall be nameless, that these commentators always kept in the most distant quarters from their principals in the lower world, through a consciousness of shame and guilt, because they had so horribly misrepresented the meaning of those authors to posterity. (*GT* III, 8, 242)

IT IS a nice irony that Gulliver's report from Glubbdubdrib applies so aptly to Swift and his commentators. They seem no less numerous than Homer's or Aristotle's and just as likely to misrepresent their 'principal'; perhaps in time to come a nameless ghost will report their shame and Swift prove as haughtily dismissive as Aristotle is of Scotus and Ramus. But even if we can bear the thought of Swift scorning our endeavours from the shades we are likely to be daunted by the sheer volume of previous commentary. What more is there to say? Hasn't everything been said already?

We may find reassurance in the thought both that *Gulliver's Travels* is virtually inexhaustible and that criticism is essentially exploratory in character: it is not in the nature of the one to yield up all its meanings at once or of the other to come to settled conclusions which remain valid for all time. What Gulliver learns of scientific theory – that new systems of nature are 'but new fashions which would vary in every age' – is true also of literary criticism. Each age will see things from a different angle and find something fresh that it needs to say. This is amply illustrated by the critical debate surrounding

Gulliver's Travels and more generally by the condition of literary criticism at the present time when radical approaches are opening up new perspectives and challenging inherited assumptions about the way in which texts communicate meaning.

We have seen that at various periods criticism of *Gulliver's Travels* has been dominated by some over-riding preoccupation and at any given time this has tended to close off other possibilities. Thus the impulse behind much of the criticism of the 1950s and 1960s was to show as false the old view of the *Travels* as 'the splenetic outburst of a man with a grudge against life' (Williams, 1958, p.9) This is how Kathleen Williams described the view that she herself countered in one of the most distinguished and influential of the interpretations published at that time. Deftly combining a sophisticated appreciation of the workings of Swift's satire with scholarly insight into the context of ideas, she contradicted the kind of judgement delivered by George Orwell, who having analysed the *Travels* with a mixture of iconoclastic energy, affection and plain common sense, concluded in general agreement with many earlier critics that the book's world-view 'only just passes the test of sanity' (Orwell, 1970, p.261). For Williams, however, it embodied not an imbalance verging on insanity but its opposite: in her reading Swift is the advocate of the reasonable middle way who leads his reader to recognise that the truth lies between extremes, just as Captain de Mendez, the Lord Munodi or the King of Brobdingnag occupy the middle ground that lies between the inhuman rationality of the Houyhnhnms and the subhuman degeneracy of the Yahoos. At the time this was just what readers tired of the traditional denunciations wanted to hear, but more recent criticism shifts the ground again – by emphasising rather than explaining away Swift's extremism (seen most obviously in the fantasy of institutionalised cannibalism in *A Modest Proposal*) and in emphasising the book's openness to interpretation. The first aspect is summed up by Robert C. Elliott when he says that Swift 'thinks himself into the heart of evil, traffics with impermissible', the second by Patrick Reilly who speaks of the *Travels* as 'Janus-faced, forever offering an alternative reading'.

Just as the preoccupations of a particular time can have the effect of closing off other possibilities, so also a particular kind of approach may become constricting. In spite of their conflicting conclusions, Orwell and Williams have one assumption in common: they assume that *Gulliver's Travels* comes to conclusions. Orwell, in his pursuit of Swift's 'positives', draws out a few of the interwoven strands and takes them for the whole. Williams carefully avoids any such simplification: 'the full meaning of this last book is not in any one figure but in the interrelation of them all' (Houyhnhnm, Yahoo, Gulliver, de Mendez (p.217)); nonetheless she is confident that 'Swift has not failed in his task of making his meaning clear to the candid reader'. In several ways this kind of certainty now seems less tenable. We might note, for instance, J. A. Downie's comment that, 'having supplied the text, [Swift] challenges the reader to interpret his signs' (1984, p.273). It is not merely that Williams's interpretation will not suit every reader in what it includes or emphasises but that it exhibits, though not to the same extent as Orwell's, a tendency towards what J. Hillis Miller calls 'premature closure'. This tendency results, says Miller, from the assumption that the meaning is going to be 'single, unified, and logically coherent' whereas, he contends, 'the best readings will be the ones which best account for the heterogeneity of the text'.

Behind Miller's words lies the modern debate in which literary theorists are calling into question all our inherited assumptions about the critical act and the nature and meaning of the literary text. Rather than entering into the specifics of that debate I wish, in what follows, to explore the text somewhat in the spirit of Miller's words – as an 'open' text which always has something at least slightly different to reveal.

The approach I shall adopt starts from a close, historically informed reading of the text during which I tried to be alert to the possible significance of particular details – to emphases, echoes, repetitions, to the kind of phrase which draws attention to itself – which might when taken together offer a clue to patterns of meaning. My eye alighted on this: 'And at last the boys and girls would venture to come and play hide and seek in my hair' (p.73), an example of what Churton Collins called Swift's 'minute diligence' and one which typifies the kind of imaginative actualisation which must help to explain the book's enduring appeal as a children's classic. It was intriguing, however, to find that even so innocent and charming a detail as this cannot be isolated from the satire. A few lines later we learn that the chief ministers play their games too, dancing and doing

the 'summerset' on the strait rope, and then when we turn the
telescope the other way about in the second voyage we find
Gulliver drawn much more perilously into children's play as a
baby stuffs him into his mouth like a dummy and a schoolboy
aims a hazel nut as big as a pumpkin at his head (pp. 130, 137).
The book's appeal as a book for children seemed, after all, not to
be a separate matter but closely related to its power as a satire.

Elsewhere I was struck by the cumulative denunciatory force
of the catalogues of occupations, vices and follies. I recognised
in these listings a stylistic feature of seventeenth-century prose
(Burton's *Anatomy of Melancholy*, for example), but this seemed
no more than an historical fact which offered no very helpful
way of experiencing or explaining their significance in this text.
At the same time, however, I found myself noting the resonance
of the word 'multiply' (there were echoes of the Bible and of Sir
William Temple) and when I linked this with the recurrent contrasts between simplicity and multiplicity or complexity I found I
was bringing into relationship ideas about language, social institutions and historical change. Other resonances took me further.
I was interested by the two alternative accounts of the origins of
the Yahoos, the stories of the two beings on a mountain top who
were delivered either biologically or by shipwreck from the sea.
There seemed to be connections here with the Book of Genesis,
Lucretius and the voyagers, all of which in their various ways
presented accounts of primitive or primeval life. (William S.
Anderson's essay 'Paradise Gained by Horace, Lost by Gulliver'
(Rawson, 1984) confirmed the relevance of the Biblical link.)

The working out of these lines of enquiry forms the substance
of much of what follows in this section. Clearly my approach
owes much to the 'history of ideas' tradition in Swift criticism,
but I hope that a few references to out of the way sources will
not impede the non-specialist reader. What is essential is not a
particular body of prior knowledge but open-minded alertness.
A more fundamental influence in the final subsection may in
fact be the 'epistemological' approach to the *Travels* which, while
often articulated by reference to particular works of philosophy
or science, depends ultimately on sharing something of the
philosopher's sense of the strangeness of reality and perception.
Impatient though he was with formal philosophy, Swift reaches
by the satirical route certain insights of a philosophical kind.
William Hazlitt said, 'he has taken a new view of human nature,

such as a being of a higher sphere might take of it' (Casebook, 1974, p.56), which anticipates the emphasis of the now very fashionable Russian formalists upon 'defamiliarisation' as the essence of art. Raman Selden sums up their view in these words: 'It is the special task of art to give us back the awareness of things which have become habitual objects of our everyday awareness'. He goes on to quote Tomashevsky who says of Gulliver's conversations with the Houyhnhnm: 'Compelled to tell everything with the utmost accuracy, he removes the shell of euphemistic phrases and fictitious traditions which justify such things as war, class, strife, parliamentary intrigue and so on. Stripped of their verbal justification and thus defamiliarised, these topics emerge in all their horror.' This identifies only the most direct way in which Swift defamiliarises the world. Ultimately everything in the book serves the same purpose, of re-presenting the world in order to restore its strangeness.

In emphasising this aspect of the book and its openness to interpretation my discussion of the *Travels* differs in one respect from those accounts which interpret it as a kind of treatise. It may be argued that in belonging, as in some measure it does, to the literature of ideas and argument, *Gulliver's Travels* is to be expected to yield a more or less systematic set of doctrines in much the same way as didactic or propagandist writings in politics or morality. There is no doubt that in certain of his works Swift wrote in this way and with these ends in view. And satire has often been defined as if it were intended to achieve certain direct ends of a reformative kind. But it is significant that Swift distances himself from any such reading of the *Travels* by pointing up Gulliver's absurdly specific reformative expectations: 'Behold, after above six months' warning, I cannot learn that my book hath produced one single effect according to my intentions'. No one is likely to believe that in the matter of particular outcomes ('Smithfield blazing with pyramids of law-books', 'the physicians banished', etc.) Swift actually shared Gulliver's disappointment. He had another and less ambitious end in view: 'to vex the world'. In the *Oxford English Dictionary's* definition 'vex' suggests quite precisely what in Swift's hands the satirical process is actually like: 'to trouble, afflict, or harass (a person, etc.) by aggression, encroachment, or other interference with peace and quiet.' To read the book in this light is not to deny it a 'serious' purpose but only to acknowledge that it attains its purpose through the reader's total experience of engaging with the text rather than by the reception of a readily encapsulated 'message'. To say this is only to say that ultimately *Gulliver's Travels* belongs to the realm of imaginative literature rather than to that of philosophical or moralistic discourse. Unlike works which rely upon a logical ordering of propositions it does not fail if its conclusions remain problematic. After all, it is only Gulliver who believes he has a simple message for the world and even he professes a willingness to 'leave the judicious reader to his own remarks and applications' (p.341).

The 'openness' of our text is amply demonstrated by the range of possible readings that remain credible and current at the present time. It is a book of many kinds: a novel, a picaresque novel, a near-novel, not a novel at all; an ethical tract, a politico-sociological treatise; a parody, a supreme example of the satirist's art, a tragic work, a comic masterpiece, a children's classic. It is a book about human nature; about politics and power, about human history; about the nature of societies and institutions; about science and learning; about the ways of knowing, experiencing, perceiving the world. It is, moreover, still in some sense a book about Swift; and one might add, bearing in mind what it shares with Sterne's *Tristram Shandy*, that it is a book about books, about the ways of language, a book about itself.

Some of these possibilities have dominated the debate; some have been pursued almost to the point of exhaustion. At least one, once dominant, is now being recovered. The renewed discussion of Swift's presence in the text is a reminder that the older and cruder treatments of the subject are not all that remains to be said. Gulliver's disenchantment with rulers and politicians and his withdrawal and alienation at the end of the book echo moods and moments in his own life too closely for them to be disregarded. The ambivalences of the text are Swift's own: of a man with an authoritarian cast of mind who served liberty, who ridiculed science but absorbed the insights of scientific discovery into his own vision of the world, who affected to disdain princes and courtiers but who found satisfaction in their friendship and approval. Yeats's statement remains pregnant with possibilities: 'Swift seemed to shape his narrative upon some clairvoyant vision of his own life.'

There are matters here which deserve further discussion but of the possibilities I have identified I shall here consider only three: *Gulliver's Travels* as a children's classic, as a book about human history, and as a book about language and books.

A children's classic?

It may be helpful to begin by recalling two of the valuable points made by Angus Ross in his short study of *Gulliver's Travels* (1968). He suggests that if the book is deficient as a work of fiction it is because its imaginative centre is not the narrative itself but *argument*. This leads him to associate it not with the mainstream of prose fiction, nor with works of formal philosophy, but with works such as *Paradise Lost*, More's *Utopia* and Johnson's *Rasselas*, which, combining fictionality with abstract discourse, 'imaginatively present views of the world to thinking men'. He acknowledges however, that the *Travels* also appeals to the part of us which is 'satisfied by fairy tales, by eyes as big as saucers, by the bean-stalk or by Pinocchio's nose growing inexorably longer, like a tree twig' (p.21). In Ross's account there may be a tension but ultimately no contradiction between the presentation of ideas and the telling of a captivating story, for the second subserves the first by endowing the argument with dramatic and symbolic significance – a fact which he underlines in his close readings of the text. The two aspects are not always held in balance so carefully: the ideas are so absorbing and their working out so complex, that there is always the danger that when we write about it (though not as we read it) we shall neglect the book's quality as a work of the fictional imagination and thus leave out of account an important constituent of the experience of reading it. What I would wish to reaffirm is that Swift's skill and ingenuity in the detailed working out of his narrative are not incidental to his main design but essential elements of his vision and his strategy. One way of developing this point is by taking up Ross's hint about the bean-stalk and Pinocchio.

That a disturbing satire should have taken its place among the children's classics has often been noted, but usually only as an amusing paradox of no real critical significance. After all, it could be said, *Gulliver's Travels* as a children's classic is not what the adult reader turns to; it is a different book altogether, a truncated version typically consisting only of the first or of the first and second voyages, embellished with illustrations of

Gulliver tied to the ground or looming waistcoated over the rooftops of the Lilliputian capital. But even the way in which the situations these illustrations depict have lodged themselves in the imagination to reappear as familiar archetypes for cartoonist and advertiser suggests that their power goes beyond the decorative charm of a toylike world. John Traugott's 'The Yahoo in the Doll's House: *Gulliver's Travels* the Children's Classic' (Rawson, 1984) explains the power by suggesting, with reference to Piaget's psychology of childhood, that what Swift presents in *Gulliver's Travels* is a re-enactment of the games, fears and fantasies of childhood in which, to quote one example, the adult plays passive victim to the child and then in a sudden role reversal rises as monster to terrorise the child. The roles and situations are various and change with great fluidity. Thus Gulliver is variously the pinioned or terrorising giant, the child, and a doll or clock-work toy. At times he is like a child at play with toys and dolls, the source of power and authority in a world created in unconsciously satirical imitation of the externals and uncomprehended rituals of the adult world. At other times he is the child or the doll, made puny and vulnerable by his small size, winning approval or recognition by playing up to his controllers' expectations of him.

It is clear that what is most powerful in children's stories, as in children's play, corresponds in profound ways with deep-seated needs, impulses and anxieties. One set of needs is fulfilled when play is used educatively as a means by which the child accustoms and accommodates itself to the conventions of the adult world. Other aspects of play may take the opposite direction and demonstrate the child's freedom from, indeed rebellion against, these encroaching conventions, seeing the world in ways and enacting possibilities which are conventionally unacceptable. Thus, beyond their superficial charm, we find in children's stories not only patterns of approved conduct but a celebration of what is subversive of those patterns. This may take the form of descriptions of children eluding adult authority, but it may also venture into a fantasy world which entertains 'naughty' possibilities. The tale of Tom Thumb is in part at least a story of this type. From the fact that he himself mentions it mock-seriously in *A Tale of a Tub* and that it was used for satirical reference by Henry Fielding and other contemporaries, it seems likely that it was in Swift's mind as he wrote the *Travels*. The point of referring to it here is not, however, to engage in source study (although I would claim it as a source), but to illustrate an aspect of the *Travels* which it shares with children's stories.

Iona and Peter Opie, who have made available to modern readers the text of a seventeenth-century chapbook edition of *Tom Thumb* such as Swift might have known, suggest that it appeals as a glorious idea rich in imaginative possibilities rather than a literary masterpiece (*The Classic Fairy Tales*, 1974). Even so, many of the details in the chapbook text are like anticipations of details in the *Travels*. Such is the disproportion between Tom and the normal scale of things that ingenious adaptation of the finest textures and finest objects is necessary to clothe him and provide for him. Leaves, cobwebs, thistledown, apple-rind, mouse-skin, and human hairs are the materials for his garments. A chair and a coach are made from walnut shells, the latter with button-moulds for wheels, and he boasts that he can use an egg-shell as a boat. In much the same way Gulliver uses shaving stubble to make a comb, human hair to weave chair seats and a purse, although his wants are also supplied by craftsmen who turn out miniature furniture and utensils which remind Gulliver of doll's house fittings in a London toyshop. For Tom, as for Gulliver, the world is full of perils: he is imprisoned in a pin-box (a fate such as a sylph might suffer in Pope's *Rape of the Lock*) and is swallowed by a cow, a giant and a fish. Three incidents in particular resemble Gulliver's adventures. Tom falls into a bowl of pudding batter just as Gulliver is dropped into a bowl of cream; having been swallowed by the cow he is discharged in a cow-pat (recalling Gulliver's misadventure, *GT* 164), and he is taken up into the air by a raven, a device which, suitably adapted, Swift uses as the climax to the second voyage.

There are moments of glory too. Like Gulliver, Tom is specially favoured by the King, travels with him and is constantly in his company, and as his fame spreads people come from all parts of the kingdom to see him. Tom's previous position of servitude in the giant's castle foreshadows Gulliver's unhappy days as a slave performer ruthlessly exploited by the giant farmer before he too becomes a court favourite. At the court Tom's familiarity with the gentlewomen and maids of honour there anticipates Gulliver's experience at the court of the King of Brobdingnag:

> For his company was so pleasing, that many times they gave him leave to sleep upon their knees, and now and then in their pockets, with many

> such like private places, and withal to sit upon their pin pillows and play
> with their pins, and to run at tilt against their bosoms with a bull-rush;
> for bigger weapon was he not able to manage. (*spelling modernised*)

In actualising Tom's situation so vividly and investing it, however
nebulously, with double entendre, this teeters on the edge
of impropriety. The satirical impulse in the corresponding
passages in *Gulliver's Travels* ensures that they are more explicit
in what they reveal and more emphatic in their moral inferences: 'They would often strip me naked from top to toe,
and lay me at full length in their bosoms; wherewith I was
much disgusted' (p.157). But in each case it is evident that
once the creative imagination is at work there can be no
certainty that fanciful transformations and changes of scale
will remain safe and charming. The image of a manikin
in a ladies' chamber is too suggestive to be entirely innocent.

The effects Swift achieves through minification and magni-
fication are of various kinds, not all of them pointedly satirical
or heavily moral. The malevolent old miser in spectacles whose
eyes appeared like the full moon shining into a chamber at two
windows is described with the mischievous wonder of fairy tale
and he is like those foolish giants who are both to be feared and
laughed at. Later in the second voyage the image of Gulliver's
sailing boat wafted by the 'gale' (a familiar eighteenth-century
poeticism for 'breeze') from the ladies' fans lends the passage
a decorative charm akin to Pope's descriptions of the sylphs
in the *Rape of the Lock*. There is scientific wonderment too:
the safe distances of the miniature give rise to such delightful
touches in the first voyage as 'a young girl threading an invisible
needle with invisible silk' (p.93), but these give way in the second
voyage to gruesome magnifications in which Gulliver sees flies
leaving 'their loathsome excrement or spawn' on his food and
'that viscous matter, which our naturalists tell us, enables those
creatures to walk with their feet upwards upon a ceiling' (p.148).
Whereas the children of Lilliput played hide and seek in his
hair, Gulliver can now see lice on people's clothes, rooting with
their snouts like swine (p.152). Reduced to the level of a small
animal, Gulliver is himself repellent and frightens the farmer's
wife who 'screamed and ran back as women in England do at
the sight of a toad or a spider' (p.127). Gulliver, representative
of Man, the measure of all things, can now use his physical
proportions to illustrate the size of bodily cavities and by a

horrific imaginative leap imagine himself entering therein: 'There was a woman with a cancer in her breast, swelled to a monstrous size, full of holes, in two or three of which I could have easily crept, and covered my whole body' (p.151).

One way of explaining what happens is to say that we enter, or re-enter, with Gulliver a childhood world of conjectural possibilities in which we rehearse in fantasy what could happen given certain improbable shifts of situation or circumstance. It is the world of 'What if . . .?' What if you were a giant (as you might seem to your dolls and toys)? Where would you relieve yourself? And who would clear up the mess? When you stand with legs astride to make a triumphal arch, what about that embarrassing hole in the crotch of your trousers? And just imagine putting out a fire in the doll's house! Returning to normal size, what if rats were the size of dogs and flies the size of eagles? What if a giant monkey kidnapped you and fed you as her child? What if one were small enough to sit astride a nipple or enter a bodily cavity? Which cavity? Possibilities of this kind, which set aside considerations of practicality, probability and respectability are part of the imaginative life of children. As the child is inducted into adult life such thoughts tend to be censored out or pushed to the margins of the mind – if not, the individual is likely to be regarded as immature. But the satirist may reawaken the old free-ranging fantasy in order to renew our sense of the strange and questionable nature of the supposedly normal and predictable world to which we have become habituated. Part of our delight in reading *Gulliver's Travels* is a sense of liberation as we follow Swift in the free play of his imagination and rediscover the world from a new angle. But Swift carries us, thus liberated, to startling conclusions, not always because he is so explicit that he 'leaves nothing to the imagination' but because he leaves us with some of the imagining to do. This much-quoted sentence from *A Tale of a Tub* is an example of how he does this by ironic under-statement: 'Last Week I saw a Woman *flay'd*, and you will hardly believe, how much it altered her Person for the worse.' In the Voyage to Brobdingnag he draws a veil out of respect for our and his own sensitivity: 'The handsomest among these Maids of Honour, a pleasant frolicsome girl of sixteen, would sometimes set me astride upon one of her nipples, with many other tricks, wherein the reader will excuse me for not being over particular' (p.158).

For Gulliver the conjectural possibilities become an inescapable reality and form part of a pattern of events which he must live through. This places Gulliver under pressure, a pressure which, from a normal readerly tendency to identify with a protagonist, we share. It originates in simple situations of physical danger or embarrassment for as Freud said, a comic situation 'is largely based on embarrassment in which we feel again the helplessness of the child'. Children, often acutely self-conscious, might readily sympathise with Gulliver's awkwardness about his lavatorial arrangments:

> I was pressed to do more than one thing, which another could not do for me, and therefore endeavoured to make my mistress understand that I desired to be set down on the floor; which after she had done, my bashfulness would not suffer me to express myself farther than pointing to the door, and bowing several times. The good woman with much difficulty at last perceived what I would be at, and taking me up again in her hand, walked into the garden where she set me down. I went on one side about two hundred yards, and beckoning to her not to look or to follow me, I hid myself between two leaves of sorrel, and there discharged the necessities of nature. (II.i.132–3)

Only when the moment of relief comes can he actually say 'what he would be at'!

The first two voyages, above all the second, are particularly rich in such situations in which we empathise with Gulliver's danger or embarrassment. They are less frequent, though not absent, in the third voyage (a fact which may explain the relative flatness of that section), but they return in a few moments of considerable power in the final voyage. Gulliver's pathetic concern, in the face of the Houyhnhnms' insistence that he is a Yahoo, to cling to whatever will preserve his distinctiveness, means that he prefers (like an uneasy guest) to keep his gloves on and results in the embarrassing incident when (like a child away from home) his bedcoverings fall off to reveal him naked. We see him defiled and mobbed by the Yahoos who treat him with the contempt of birds for a tame jackdaw and, most embarrassingly of all, he becomes the object of a female Yahoo's lust, which 'was a matter of diversion to my master and his family, as well as of mortification to myself': 'She embraced me after a most fulsome manner; I roared as loud as I could, and the nag came galloping towards me, whereupon she quitted her grasp, with the utmost reluctancy, and leaped upon the opposite bank, where she stood gazing and howling all the time I was putting on my clothes' (pp. 314–15). Gulliver's predicament throughout the fourth voyage is that of a human being lodged in an ape-house. That he should, against Houyhnhnm persuasion (it has been called brainwashing), have to make such an effort to maintain his identity and his dignity (rather as he tries to do in Brobdingnag when he is treated as a small animal) generates deep unease and embarrassment which communicate themselves to the reader. But as is usual in comic situations of mistaken identity, to know the truth does not relieve the embarrassment. It is easy to show that Gulliver's discomfiture is mankind's and that it is Swift's way of making a general point about human pride. But it may be limiting to concentrate too narrowly upon translating such incidents into moral doctrine. The fictional experiences of Gulliver remain in the imagination to inform our sense of our relationship with the world. To share those experiences is, in some way, to share the free imagination of the child, who imagines more than he admits and asks more difficult questions than adults are usually ready to answer.

Worlds past and present

Hugh Kenner, depicting Gulliver as a shallow modern empiricist, says that he 'has no notion of what the past has to teach' (Donoghue, 1971, p.426). Had he known the classics he would surely have recognised resemblances between the Brobdingnagians and the Cyclops, between the Struldbruggs and Tithonus and the Sibyl of Cumae, between the Houyhnhnms and the wise Centaurs. These things are closed to him and history interests him instead as an entertaining spectacle or a string of surprising facts. The limitation Kenner wittily exposes can be overstated: it is Gulliver's, not the book's. Indeed, the past is continually recalled in the *Travels* and an historical frame of reference is essential to many of its satirical insights.

Gulliver has much to report about the past and Swift gives him some insight into the processes of historical change. He reports the history of the religious and political divisions in Lilliput (reflecting English history from the Reformation onwards, pp.84 ff.). He gives the King of Brobdingnag an account of England in the last century, which provokes the King's condemnation: 'an heap of conspiracies, rebellions, murders, massacres, revolutions, banishments' (p. 172). He reads the history of Brobdingnag and of the past struggles between king, nobility and people, and then in Glubbdubdrib, like Dr Faustus, calls upon famous personages and incidents from the past (chapters 7 and 8). When later in the third voyage he imagines having a Struldbrugg's immortality he rhapsodizes about witnessing the unfolding of the historical process over hundreds of years, remarking 'the several Gradations by which Corruption steals into the World' and seeing:

> The various revolutions of states and empires; the changes in the lower and upper world; ancient cities in ruins, and obscure villages become the seats of kings. Famous rivers lessening into shallow brooks, the ocean leaving one coast dry, and overwhelming another: the discovery of many countries yet unknown. Barbarity overrunning the politest nations, and the most barbarous becoming civilized. I should then see the discovering of the *longitude*, the *perpetual motion*, the *universal medicine*, and many other great inventions brought to the utmost perfection. (III, x, 255)

Gulliver shares contemporary optimism in expecting science in its relentless advance to achieve things which were then by-words for the unattainable. In other respects this passage suggests no uniform pattern of historical change but rather the alternation of rise and fall, a condition of flux in which nothing has permanency but in which as the wheel turns barbarism encroaches or recedes. It is an important passage in revealing Swift's sense of pattern and change in history and his interest (perhaps stimulated by the historical ruminations of Sir William Temple) in the remote as well as the recent. History in *Gulliver's Travels* is not confined entirely to the specifics of the immediate past with incidental references to famous figures from ancient Greece and Rome; it is framed by a larger sense, which Gulliver himself may not share, of the unfolding pattern since the Creation. The sense of all human history as a manageable whole was perhaps greater in an age which could date the Creation with precision (4004 BC according to one account), with the result that events such as the Fall, Noah's Flood or the building of the Tower of Babel could be placed in the same date-list as the execution of Charles I or the battle of Blenheim.

What Gulliver usually discovers or assumes is not flux but relentless decline. (Even the Brobdingnagians, we learn, are small and weak by comparison with their forebears, p.178). Indeed, at the heart of the book, as one of a set of assumptions which direct its satire, is a view of human history as a degenerative process which through corruption and complication (the 'multiplying' tendency) carries mankind away from primal virtues and simplicities. It is a view common in earlier ages (as in the traditional idea that time begins with the Age of Gold), but it was already in retreat in Swift's lifetime. The notion of progress as the underlying dynamic in human history was becoming established and issued earlier in the century in optimistic forecasts of scientific advance and later in sweeping assertions such as Turgot's: 'the human race . . . marches always, although slowly, towards still higher perfection' (1750; Stanley Pollard, *The Idea of Progress*, 1971, p.7). To Swift such a view would have seemed not merely facile but absolutely false, as we can see from his 'Thoughts on Religion', where having recalled the creation of Adam and Eve, their Fall and loss of supremacy over the beasts, he concludes: 'But men [unlike the animals] degenerate every day, merely by the folly, the perverseness, the avarice, the tyranny, the pride, the treachery, or inhumanity of their own kind.' At many points *Gulliver's Travels* restates and enacts this view. Gulliver notes that the original laws of Lilliput have been overtaken by 'the most scandalous Corruptions into which these People are fallen by the degenerate Nature of Man' (p.96). In Glubbdubdrib Gulliver reflects with melancholy 'how much the Race of human Kind was degenerate among us, within these Hundred Years past'. As has often been noted, even the circumstances (shipwreck, desertion, piracy, mutiny), which lead voyage by voyage to Gulliver's separation from his shipmates successively reveal darker aspects of human nature.

The juxtaposition of the third and fourth voyages is of crucial significance in giving shape and interconnection to what might without it be merely a series of disconnected references to decline and degeneration. The third voyage, through a series of thinly concealed descriptions of eighteenth-century science, manners and politics provides a satirical portrait of modern society which has reached an extreme point of sophistication at which it appears no longer capable of ordinary competence in managing its everyday affairs. This describes what for Swift was the modern world and is set in direct contrast to a simple, non-technological society which has preserved unchanged the features of a primitive civilisation. In the third voyage, where people go in dread of the apocalypse, we are haunted also by the Struldbruggs who, in their morose and mindless vacuity, symbolise the old age of the world. The Houyhnhnms, in contrast, live in a land which retains the vigour, freshness and simplicity of an early or newly created culture. Between these two chronological and cultural extremes, the earliest and the latest, the simplest and the most sophisticated, we assume an ongoing process of change which we are able to glimpse in incidental references to the more immediate past and the formative tensions which have progressively transformed the several societies to which we are introduced.

Houyhnhnmland takes us back in imagination to a society which while apparently quite functional has not led to a proliferation of duties, offices, commodities, desires and which remains true to its own first principles. If nothing else, it provides us with a vision of essential societal needs by which we can measure the alternatives. It is a society without letters, dependent for knowledge upon oral tradition, with enough understanding of astronomy to calculate years, months and eclipses, living in simple but weatherproof buildings and making use of flint tools. The Houyhnhnms are healthy and engage in athletic exercises to develop strength, speed and endurance. They regulate their conduct in matters of marriage, breeding and governance according to simple traditional rules which are not the subject of discussion or revision.

The contrast between Houyhnhnm society and that of Laputa and Lagado could scarcely be more striking. Within the *Travels* Laputa represents the outcome of the assumed historical process which leads from a simple, basic existence as found in Houyhnhnmland by way of invention, manufacture and sophistication to a society of extreme complexity and artificiality. It represents the condition of modern society as condemned by the Houyhnhnm who alleges, reports Gulliver: 'That we . . . had been very successful in multiplying our original wants, and seemed to spend our whole lives in vain endeavours to supply them by our own inventions' (IV.vii.306). The most basic things and functions are elaborated beyond any real need as if in perverse pursuit of novelty: meats are cut in the shape of mathematical figures, speaking and listening can only continue with constant artificial assistance from the flappers, the people 'are under continual disquietudes, never enjoying a minute's peace of mind' from the fear they have of planetary collisions and other celestial mishaps, but they are incompetent in making clothes and in building. In Lagado many of the same tendencies are apparent: a desire to be novel at any price, especially, it seems, if this involves the abandonment of tried and tested ways or the perverse application of manifestly unsuitable means to the task in hand – such as the use of a blind man to distinguish colours. The contrast Swift presents between Lagado and the estate of Lord Munodi points up the kind of degeneration through pointless innovation which he is obviously concerned to embody in these fictions. In the town he sees strangely built houses in disrepair and people in rags walking hurriedly with 'their eyes fixed' (p.219) while in the country he finds the soil ill-cultivated, the houses ill-contrived and ruinous and the people in a state of misery and want. But as he approaches the estate of Munodi 'the scene was wholly altered; we came into a most beautiful country; farmers' houses at small distances, neatly built, the fields enclosed, containing vineyards, corn-grounds and meadows. Neither do I remember to have seen a more delightful prospect' (p.220). This well-regulated landscape and the social order it portrays stand between the primitivism of the Houyhnhnms, who grow oats in woodland clearings, and the disastrous innovation of the Lagadans. It is a rare glimpse, in Swift, of an attainable modern ideal expressed in terms which may recall Pope's much more enthusiastic celebration of landscape and social well-being in the modern world. It is a reminder also of the force of Kathleen Williams's argument that Swift is an advocate of the middle way.

For much of the time, however, Swift directs our thoughts to earlier stages in human history. In presenting Houyhnhnmland he blends contrasting accounts of the origins of mankind and the nature of primitive human societies. Ian Higgins has shown that Houyhnhnm culture closely resembles that of ancient Sparta, but this need not exclude other parallels. Swift left on record his view that 'the Scripture-system of man's creation, is what Christians are bound to believe'. According to this, God created Adam and Eve as the parents of mankind, placing them in the Garden of Eden where they enjoyed power and supremacy over the animals and from which they were expelled for eating the forbidden fruit. A quite different, non-Christian account would have been known to Swift in Lucretius, who describes the

creation of vegetable, animal and human life through a process
of spontaneous generation in which the heat and moisture of the
soil generated 'wombs' which matured and gave birth to living
forms. According to Lucretius the early human beings were big-
ger and tougher than modern man, relatively insensitive to heat
and cold, subsisting upon what nature provided without even
the basic elements of a civilised life: agriculture, fire, articulate
speech, clothing, houses or the restraints of morals and laws.
(Up to this point they do not rise above the level of the Yahoos.)
However, in due course human beings began to build huts and
to use skins and fire, marital unions were formed, neighbours
entered into alliances and articulate speech developed. At a
later stage new inventions were made, kings began to found
cities, the notions of property and the use of gold for monetary
transactions were discovered and men craved for fame and
power. Then the kings were killed and after a period of mob
rule mankind began to live within an orderly framework of laws
and institutions. The account presented by Diodorus Siculus is
in many respects similar and he too stresses the wretchedness of
early man: they 'led a wretched existence having no clothing to
cover them, knowing not the use of dwelling and fire, and also
being totally ignorant of cultivated food'. Thus whereas in the
Biblical account man is created by the hand of God and placed
in a state of peace, plenty and innocence which he forfeits
for a life of toil and sorrow, in Lucretius and Diodorus
man begins in wretchedness and develops towards a better life.

Swift introduced into *Gulliver's Travels* two explanations of the
presence of the Yahoos in Houyhnhnmland which correspond
in certain ways with these two accounts. Houyhnhnm tradition
has it that 'many years ago, two or three brutes appeared
together upon a mountain, whether produced by the heat
of the sun upon corrupted mud and slime, or from the
ooze and froth of the sea, was never known. ... These
Yahoos engendered, and their brood in a short time grew so
numerous as to overrun and infest the whole nation' (p.319).
Using new knowledge gained from Gulliver and the example
of Gulliver's own arrival in that country, the Houyhnhnm
master suggests an alternative explanation: the two Yahoos
'had been driven thither over the sea; that coming to land,
and being forsaken by their companions, they retired to the
mountains, and degenerating by degrees, became in process

of time, much more savage than those of their own species in the country from whence these two originals came' (p.320).

The first account follows Lucretius since it assumes that new species can come into being by a process of spontaneous generation. It thus gives the Yahoos their own separate origins and it is merely a biological accident that they closely resemble humankind. If this is so then the Houyhnhnms are mistaken in believing Gulliver and the Yahoos to be from the same stock and, whatever the resemblances, Gulliver's initial instinct is right – to resist identification with them. The second account, however, confirms what the pressure of circumstance has convinced Gulliver to be the case: he and the Yahoos *are* members of the same species.

The two original Yahoos, it now becomes clear, were human beings who suffered a misfortune (abandonment or shipwreck) similar to Gulliver's or Robinson Crusoe's. They are evidently from a technologically advanced civilisation in that they appear to have arrived at the shores of Houyhnhnmland in an ocean-going ship, which makes their relationship to Gulliver and ourselves closer and more disturbing. In our imaginative experience of the book it establishes his and our kinship with them (which is underlined by the female Yahoo's sexual attraction, p.314), with the insidious implication that what the Yahoos are we might become.

Changes in behaviour, such as the reversion to barbarism of the boys in William Golding's *Lord of the Flies*, may seem inherently more probable in those marooned on an island than actual physical changes which might turn a ship's captain into a capering ape. However, lurking in the background to *Gulliver's Travels* are certain stories about the degeneration of human beings, isolated from their kind, towards a Yahoo-like animality. Stories of Peter the Wildman, lost as a child in the woods, were circulating at about the time the *Travels* was published, and Swift would also have known of Edward Tyson's studies of apes and men. In *Orang Outang, sive Homo Silvestris* (1699) Tyson documents his anatomical examination of a man-like ape in which he discovers 'the nexus of animal and rational', the point at which the human and animal seem to converge. And Tyson supplemented his study with a collection of anecdotes from many ancient and modern sources about man and the simians. He cites the case of a woman on an island who mates with apes and tells the story of Peter Serrano, a castaway who having managed to survive for three years, 'the Hairs of his Body grew in that manner, that he was covered all over with Bristles; the hair of his Head and Beard reaching his Waste, that he appeared like some Wild or Savage Creature'. Since the Yahoos' hairiness is a sign of their animality this detail may be significant.

The behavioural patterns of the Yahoos are embryonic versions of the activities of civilised beings. Their main purpose is obviously satirical but once the Yahoos are seen as the descendants of seafarers from 'our' world their actions become the pathetic vestigial reminders of what we share with them. It is as if Swift is again asking a question of the 'What if . . .?' type: What if a man and a woman were marooned on an island? The situation might issue in an idyll, but in Swift's hands, perhaps with Tyson's strange documentation in mind, the outcome is a satirical grotesque which calls up an ancient dread of the unholy mingling of animal and human.

The Yahoos, themselves descendants of outcasts from Eden, are intruders in another Garden, the land of the Houyhnhnms. Now like beasts themselves, they are abhorred by all the animals (p.389), just as God ordained that fallen man would be 'cursed above all cattle, and above every beast of the field' (Genesis 3.14). By a process of degeneration they have arrived at a state similar to that of the first men in the accounts of Lucretius and Diodorus Siculus or of savages in the records of travellers in Swift's own day. The Houyhnhnms, on the other hand, present a view of primitive life which bears a significant resemblance to Eden or more particularly myths of the Golden Age found in other classical sources such as Hesiod:

> As gods they were wont to live, with a life void of care, apart from, and without labour and trouble: nor was wretched old age at all impending, but, ever the same in hands and feet did they delight themselves in festivals out of reach of all ills: and they died, as if o'ercome by sleep; all blessings were theirs; of its own will the fruitful field would bear them fruit, much and ample and they gladly used to reap the labours of their hands in quietness among many good things, being rich in flocks, and dear to the blessed gods. (J. Banks, *The Works of Hesiod*, 1856, p.80)

This happy world blessed by gods is certainly rosier than the godless world of the joylessly contented Houyhnhnms, where the inclusion of such realities as a class system with regulated hours for labourers creates the impression of austere practicality far removed from the spontaneous happiness of most paradises. But it shares with Hesiod's Golden Age exemption from want, care, the wretchedness of old age and the anguish of dying and though, indeed, a drab paradise, it is, for the purposes of contrast with the unseemly squalour and servitude of the Yahoos, a sort of Eden. If it is accepted as such one might see the fourth voyage as a wry postscript to the Biblical story of the Fall. As Swift reminds us in the passage already quoted, Adam and Eve, having sinned, lost their supremacy over the animals and are sent into exile from Eden. It is a fitting ironic reversal that, describing our fallen world as it has become since their days, Swift should discover to us a land where beasts now have supremacy and where the degenerate descendants of Adam and Eve are not merely not supreme but are placed in servitude to ruling beasts. The Houyhnhnms, like Adam and Eve *before* the Fall, are not ashamed of their nakedness and do not know good and evil. Into their Eden comes Gulliver, an interloper from the fallen world. To cover his nakedness he is reduced, like Adam and Eve, to making garments from skins and he has endless accounts to give of the evil deeds of men. Steward Lacasce (1970) has gone so far as to say that his presence is like Satan's in Eden: through contact with him his Houyhnhnm master begins to fall into human kinds of error and deceit (for example in concealing the truth about Gulliver). But the garden must be preserved from evil and just as Adam and Eve were cast out of Eden so must Gulliver be banished.

In calling to mind these potent myths of creation and primitive life Swift colours his narrative with a powerful sense of what humankind has lost and what it has become. Eden is forever denied us and the patterns of conduct which led to and flowed from Adam and Eve's first sin seem still inescapably active in the world. There is no way in which Gulliver or anyone, within the Christian scheme of things, can resign from the human race or renounce his share in the collective inheritance of original sin, as the absurdity of Gulliver's desire to do so makes clear. Nor is there any way in which he can regain Eden for, as the example of the Yahoos' ancestors has demonstrated and as the Houyhnhnms fear that Gulliver would in his turn demonstrate, each man carries within himself the seeds which will destroy Eden. Banished from Eden in the beginnings of time Adam and Eve and their offspring proceeded to multiply in number, folly and wickedness. A new start after Noah's flood only began the process again, and this was in turn re-enacted when the Yahoos' ancestors arrived in Houyhnhnmland, just as Gulliver's banishment and sad departure are a comic re-enactment of the first departure from Eden.

Gulliver's Travels presents a satirical record of the process as it has run on through time. There is no way forward and at the conclusion of his *Travels* Gulliver is at a dead end. Shut out of Eden he can but try to reconcile himself to reality: to 'habituate' himself to the sight of a human creature and to allow his wife, but at the farthest end of a long table, into his presence again.

Into the world of words

If the world and all it contains awaits the writer's touch to reawaken its dormant strangeness this must include the language he uses and the book he writes. Of all the acquisitions made by mankind in its development none is more wonderful, more curious, more deeply formative of consciousness and yet more likely to be taken for granted than language and the elaborate communicative forms, conventions, techniques and artefacts into which it has evolved. *Gulliver's Travels* bears witness to this in various ways. Languages and language-learning are, for example, one of the essential ingredients of each of the voyages. The ways in which language is used and abused are an important indicator of the intellectual and moral condition of each of the lands Gulliver visits. And our attention is repeatedly drawn, through Gulliver's references to his own book and his own writing, to the strangeness of Swift's chosen way of depicting reality through an extravagant fiction which masquerades as Gulliver's plain truth and indeed, to the strangeness of writing itself. It is with this in mind that I have in this section used an unmodernised text (though with page references to the Penguin edition).

We begin in Lilliput with the impenetrable strangeness of an unknown language with Gulliver the witness to what might just as well be a dumb-show. Cries of 'Hekinah Degul' and 'Tolgo Phonac' are followed by a long speech from a ladder by a Person of Quality, 'whereof I understood not one Syllable'. Gulliver, no mean linguist, tries all the languages he knows – High and Low Dutch, Latin, French, Spanish, Italian, and Lingua Franca – 'but all to no purpose'. In a short time, however, he has made great progress in learning the language. We as readers are still at a loss but, now an insider with the confident hold on things that the possession of language gives, he is able to scatter Lilliputian words with familiar ease: *Lumos Kelmin pesso desmar Lon Emposo, Nardac, Drurr, Brundrecal, Glumgluff, Burglum, Glimigrim* (by the Blefuscudians called *Flunec*), *Snilpall*.

Once he has penetrated the language barrier Gulliver's experiences in Lilliput afford a number of significant reminders of the ways of language in a sophisticated society, chiefly in laudatory references to the King and the chilling legal language of the articles of liberty and the impeachment: 'did maliciously, traitorously, and devilishly, by the discharge of his Urine, put out the said Fire kindled in the said Apartment lying and being within the Precincts of the said Royal Palace'. The next two voyages contain certain other parodies of specialised language: nautical ('we reeft the Foresail and set him, we hawled aft the Foresheet'), scientific ('let AB represent a Line drawn Cross the Dominions of Balnibari; let the Line *c d* represent the Load-stone') and exotic ('My Tongue is in the Mouth of my Friend'). We are in Brobdingnag offered the linguistic ideals of brevity and simplicity and in Laputa perversions of these ideals in the elimination of language by the use of linguistic back-packs, the *reductio ad absurdum* of directness, or in the mystification of the simple as in the misinterpretation of the homely directness of 'Our Brother Tom has just got the Piles' according to the Anagrammatick Method: 'Resist – a Plot is brought home – The Tour.'

By contrast the language of the Houyhnhnms takes us back as if to the beginnings of time, reminding us of Adam's naming of things and recalling that stage in linguistic evolution which Diodorus Siculus describes:

> And though the sounds which they made were at first unintelligible and indistinct, yet gradually they came to give articulation to their speech, and by agreeing with one another upon symbols for each thing which presented itself to them, made known among themselves the significance which was attached to each term. But since groups of this kind arose over every part of the inhabited world, not all men had the same language, inasmuch as every group organised the elements of its speech by mere chance.   (Loeb edn, pp.29–31)

If language begins with random sounds to which meanings are then attached, the signs of the process are still apparent in the Houyhnhnms' words which, as readers-aloud know only too well, are variants of the horse's whinny. Semantically too their language is primitive, limited in range and displaying simple patterns of word formation. Inevitably the language has no expressions for things or concepts which have no place in their world. In their state of innocence only 'Yahoo' can supply the term for 'bad' and Gulliver's difficulties in explaining a complicated fallen world are immense: 'Power, Government, War, Law, Punishment, and a Thousand other Things had no Terms, wherein that Language could express them; which made the Difficulty almost insuperable to give my Master any conception of what I meant' (II.iv.291). We are given the circumlocutions to which he has to resort in defining a soldier and a lie, but we are left to imagine the verbal contortions required as he works his way through dizzying accumulations of occupations, crimes, follies and diseases, all of which must be described *ab initio*: 'Begging, Robbing, Stealing, Cheating, Pimping, Forswearing, Flattering, Suborning, Forging, Gaming, Lying, Fawning, Hectoring, Voting, Scribling, Stargazing, Poysoning, Whoring, Canting, Libelling, Free-thinking, and the like Occupations.' Catalogues such as this are a measure not only of the immensity of Gulliver's explanatory task but also, since language is the mirror of its society, of the extent to which society has deviated from the primal simplicities represented by the world of the Houyhnhnms. A myriad of new vices demands a multitude of new words; unknown vices need no words.

The most telling of all the circumlocutions is the phrase for a lie – 'the Thing which is not' – which nicely captures a world-view in which falsehood is so illogical as to be nonsensical. Gulliver's master's comments on the subject are important:

> For he argued thus; That the use of Speech was to make us understand one another, and to receive Information on Facts; now if any one *said the thing which was not*, these ends were defeated; because I cannot properly be said to understand him; and I am so far from receiving Information that he leaves me worse than in Ignorance. (IV.iv.286)

In his innocence the Houyhnhnm provides a purely logical model of language; the *Travels* presents a catalogue of examples of deviations from this ideal. The corruption of the world

manifests itself in the corruption of language which de₁
from its primal function of truth-telling. There are, for exam₁
the extravagant falsehoods of the conventional tributes to t
four-inch King of Lilliput: 'Delight and Terror of the Univers₁
Taller than the Sons of Men; whose Feet press down to the
Center, and whose Head strikes against the Sun.' There are
the declarations of the King's lenity which no one believes and
everyone fears. The scientists of Brobdingnag, called upon to
examine Gulliver, believe they have given a modern scientific
explanation whereas they have merely provided a clever new
term which advances knowledge not at all. Among politicians,
lawyers and historians a law of contraries operates: thus a chief
minister 'applies his Mind to all Uses, except the Indication
of his Mind; . . . he never tells a Truth, but with an Intent
that you should take it for a Lye; nor a Lye, but with
Design that you should take it for a Truth'. In Glubbdubdrib
Gulliver learns of the misrepresentations of the historians: 'I
found the World had been misled by prostitute Writers, to
ascribe the greatest Exploits in War to Cowards, the Wisest
Council to Fools.' And the lawyers 'prove by Words multiplied
from this Purpose, that *White* is *Black*, and *Black* is *White*'.

This last example makes two connections explicit: that in
Swift's satiric vision the multiplying of words is inseparable from
falsehood and that language follows the general 'multiplying'
tendencies of the fallen world in its departure from primal
simplicities. It is significant that abuses and abusers of language
should figure so prominently in Gulliver's catalogues of villainy
in Voyage IV. The vicious 'occupations' listed in Chapter
6 include forswearing, flattering, lying, hectoring, scribbling,
canting and libelling; and in Chapter 10 the satirical indictment is drawn not only against such as Highwaymen, Bawds,
Gamesters and Politicians but also informers who watch words
and actions or forge accusations for hire, gibers, censurers,
backbiters, controvertists and tedious talkers. By contrast, in
the conversations of the Houyhnhnms 'nothing passed but
what was useful, expressed in the fewest and most significant
Words' and 'there was no Tediousness, Heat, or Difference
of Sentiments'. This is not an entirely remote ideal, for the
Brobdingnagians cultivate a style which is 'clear, masculine,
and smooth, but not Florid; for they avoid nothing more than
multiplying unnecessary words, or using various Expressions'.

And in that country no law may exceed twenty-two words 'expressed in the most plain and simple Terms' which offer no scope for conflicting interpretations.

What makes the Brobdingnagians exceptional is that, while having all the communicative resources of a modern civilisation, they use these with rational restraint so that they do not lose their hold on essentials in a flood of falsifying words. The oral, pre-literate culture of the Houyhnhnms is safe in its time-warp from the malign consequences of the Gutenberg revolution whereas the Brobdingnagians, older and wiser in these matters than the European countries, have come to a rational accommodation with the printed word. 'They have had the Art of Printing, as well as the *Chinese*, Time out of Mind. But their Libraries are not very large; for that of the King's, which is reckoned the largest, doth not amount to above a thousand volumes.' Elsewhere in the world the multiplication of words is accelerated by means of the press. Thus Gulliver speaks of 'Pyramids of Law-Books', *hundreds* of commentators on Homer and Aristotle shamefacedly avoiding their 'Principals', *hundreds* of books on the egg controversy in Lilliput, and *thousands* of books on the art of government. With appropriate irony the *Travels* itself fuels the same tendency, prompting tribes of 'Answerers, Considerers, Observers, Reflectors, Detectors, Remarkers' to rush into print. And the Lagadan writing machine (whereby 'the most ignorant Person at a reasonable charge, and with a little bodily Labour, may write Books in Philosophy, Poetry, Politicks, Law, Mathematics and Theology, with the least Assistance from Genius or Study') gives us a futuristic glimpse of mechanisation accelerating and depersonalising the process. We can detect in all this a number of contemporary influences and concerns. The writing machine is quite evidently a satirical glance at the experiments with mechanical writing conducted by John Wilkins of the Royal Society (see Probyn, 1974). The concern that printing has opened the floodgates was shared by Pope who, writing in an ironical vein about himself and his poem *The Dunciad*, said: 'He lived in those days, when (after providence had permitted the Invention of Printing as a scourge for the Sins of the learned) Paper also became so cheap, and printers so numerous, that a deluge of authors cover'd the land.' Most significantly perhaps the *Travels* recalls and shares Sir William Temple's profound scepticism about the supposedly beneficial effects of one of the three or four key inventions of

the modern world: 'The invention of printing has not pe
multiplied books, but only the copies of them. . . . Books
be helps to learning and knowledge, and make it more comm
and diffused; but I doubt whether they are necessary ones or no
or much advance any science.' And he goes on to cite examples
of American civilisations which (like the Houyhnhnms') relied
upon oral traditions rather than written records.

Temple's discussion foreshadows Gulliver's description: 'The
Houyhnhnms have no Letters, and consequently their Knowledge is all traditional'. Viewed from the standpoint of such
pre-literate cultures, the world of the printed book with its
elaborate communicative codes and conventions is bound to
appear strange. And, in his defamiliarising way, Swift reinforces
his sense of strangeness throughout the *Travels*. There is, for
example, the Lilliputian description of Gulliver's pocket-book:
'a prodigious Bundle of white thin Substances, folded one over
another, about the Bigness of three Men, tied with a strong cable,
and marked with Black Figures; which we humbly conceive to
be writings; every Letter almost half as large as the Palm of our
Hands.' We are reminded, also in Lilliput, of the differences
of convention even within literate cultures in a passage which
recalls another of Temple's musings on other cultures: 'Their
manner of Writing is very peculiar; being neither from the
Left to the Right, like the *Europeans*; nor from the Right
to the Left like the Arabians; nor from up to down, like
the Chinese; nor from down to up, like the Cascagians; but
aslant from one Corner of the Paper to the other, like Ladies
in England.' The reader's eye must travel in the same direction
as the writer's hand and if by a childlike imaginative shift, we
imagine Gulliver (or Tom Thumb) as the reader in a giant's
library, what he needs in order to imitate the eye movements
of a 'normal' reader is a kind of 'standing ladder' with steps
each fifty foot long: 'The Book I had a Mind to read was put
up leaning against the Wall. I first mounted to the upper Step
of the Ladder, and turning my Face towards the Book, began
at the Top of the Page, and so walking to the Right and Left
about eight or ten paces according to the Length of the Lines,
till I had gotten a little below the Level of mine Eyes; and then
descending gradually till I came to the Bottom: After which I
mounted again, and began the other Page in the same Manner,
and so turned over the Leaf' (II.vii.177). But even before this,

Gulliver must, like a child, learn his alphabet, and he does so under Glumdalclitch's instruction with the aid of 'a little Book in her Pocket, not much larger than a Samson's Atlas' (over 50 cm square). To have mastered the language, the alphabet and the art of traversing the page is not enough: one must have mental powers of retention and concentration. The Struldbruggs fail in this essential 'because their Memory will not serve to carry them from the Beginning of a Sentence to the End'.

Although on several occasions Gulliver draws attention to his own reading, only one of the books he reads is described at any length. It is the 'little old treatise' which he finds in Glumdalclitch's bed chamber, a work of popular morality 'in little esteem except among Women and the Vulgar', which 'treats of the weakness of human kind'.

> This Writer went through all the usual Topicks of *European* Moralists; shewing how diminutive, contemptible, and helpless an Animal was Man in his own Nature; how unable to defend himself from the Inclemencies of the Air, or the Fury of wild Beasts: How much he was excelled by one Creature in Strength, by another in Speed, by a third in Foresight, by a fourth in Industry. He added, that Nature was degenerated in these latter declining Ages of the World, and could now produce only small abortive Births by Comparison of those in ancient times. He said, it was very reasonable to think there must have been Giants in former Ages. . . . From this Way of Reasoning the Author drew several more Applications useful in the Conduct of life, but needless here to repeat. For my own Part, I could not avoid reflecting, how universally this Talent was spread of drawing Lectures in Morality, or indeed rather Matters of Discontent and repining, from the Quarrels we raise with Nature. (II.vii.178)

On the face of it Gulliver's dismissal is so well-grounded and so tellingly formulated that it might seem to carry Swift's endorsement and to demand our consent. The little old book's themes were indeed commonplace ones in seventeenth-century moral discourses and perhaps therefore Swift is ridiculing arguments, in themselves questionable, which had become stale with repetition. But unsophisticated readers are, in Swift, more likely to have their priorities right than the learned and consciously clever and 'moral Applications useful in the Conduct of life' are not lightly to be set aside. What is even more curious is that the book's argument bears a close resemblance to some of the major themes of the *Travels*. Have we here discovered the book we are reading contained within itself? 'How diminutive contemptible and helpless an Animal was Man in his own Nature' aptly enough describes a central theme of the first two voyages and foreshadows the emphasis upon human insufficiency in the fourth. Far from being the sole prerogative of tedious moralists, reflections of this kind are given memorable expression by Montaigne. His *Apology for Raymond de Sebonde*, which scholars have regarded as one of Swift's influences, emphasises the helplessness of man in ways which recall the fourth voyage: 'we are the only animal abandoned, naked upon the bare earth . . . nor having wherewithal to arm and clothe us, but by the spoil of others'. Thus the little old treatise, a book within a book, is an imperfect mirror *and* a critique of the book which contains it. This may serve as a warning that we should not reduce *Gulliver's Travels* to a restatement of familiar pessimistic themes. In a world in which reason is problematical, 'where men can argue with Plausibility on both Sides of a Question', interpretation cannot be as simple as that.

Within this book's fictional world, the historical sequence which runs from the evolution of spoken language through the development of writing to the invention of printing and the proliferation of writers, readers and books, comes to its conclusion with Gulliver writing, Motte publishing, the gentle Reader reading and the first Answerers answering *Travels into Several Remote Nations of the World* (though we Answerers are still at it). The *Travels* does not stand aloof from the world it portrays: it is implicated in it and is itself a prime example of what it satirises. This self-referential tendency is no surprise for we have another example of the same thing in Gulliver's final stance as a man smitten with pride castigating men smitten with pride.

In the first place *Gulliver's Travels* draws attention to itself as a particular kind of publication. The book's typography, title page, maps and diagrams immediately identify it with contemporary books of travel, one of the largest and most popular categories of publication. The references in the introductory sections to the text's composition, transmission and reception (the style corrected, the book pruned of nautical details and politically dangerous passages, the manuscript delivered anonymously at night) together with Gulliver's irritable complaints about omissions, mistaken times and dates and the misspelling 'Brobdingnag', all help to give the book its air of authenticity but also exemplify the fact that in the modern world communication is attended by innumerable complications and corruptions. And in carrying promises of supplementary works and in provoking written responses the *Travels* not only sounds authentically contemporary but is seen to occasion the kind of proliferation the book appears to condemn.

Authorial business of this kind makes an important contribution to our sense of Gulliver as a character. As Zimmerman has remarked, what we observe in reading the *Travels* is not simply a man going through certain adventures but a man writing a book about them. Gulliver's authorial habits are borrowed from his real-life counterpart, Captain William Dampier, and while taking pleasure in the skill of the impersonation we also realise that in imitating Dampier Gulliver becomes an agent and advocate of the new science. His plain style, his omnivorous curiosity, his attention to observational detail are the hallmarks of a traveller who is acting, like Dampier, under the Royal Society's instructions to voyagers. And thus, as he does in *A Modest Proposal* and *A Tale of a Tub*, Swift adopts a standpoint and a voice to which he himself is antipathetic. As an acolyte of the Royal Society, Gulliver's most persistent claim is to truthfulness. He is irritated by those who 'are so bold as to think my Book of Travels a meer Fiction out of mine own Brain' and who 'have gone so far as to drop Hints, that the *Houyhnhnms* and *Yahoos* have no more Existence than the Inhabitants of Utopia'. And if we should find him a trifle dull, this is because he is no mere entertainer:

> I could perhaps like others have astonished thee with strange improbable Tales; but I rather chose to relate plain Matter of Fact in the simplest Manner and Style; because my principal Design was to inform, and not to amuse thee.

In one sense this is a typical piece of ironical topsyturvydom: that in giving us giants and midgets, a flying island, people who do not die, man-apes and talking horses Gulliver should have the effrontery to claim kinship with the writers of scientific travel books and behave as if superior to those mere entertainers who deal in improbable oddities and wonders. At the same time, however, we may reflect that in reading the *Travels* we are continually colliding with some extremely uncomfortable matters of fact about our world – its grossness, extravagancies and injustices, its falsehoods, follies and cruelties. On the surface there is an entertaining period piece, a transaction in the manner of Grub Street, between Lemuel Gulliver and an imaginary reading public, in the person of the 'gentle Reader', which belongs to the book's fiction; but secreted within is a transaction between Swift and ourselves, a transaction which restores strangeness to all kinds of things – and these include even the act of reading and responding to his words.

References and Further Reading

Collection of essays

References to collections of essays are normally by editor, except in the case of Richard Gravil's anthology, a companion volume to this series, which is given simply as *Casebook*.

Clifford, James L. (ed.), *Eighteenth Century English Literature: Modern Essays in Criticism* (New York, 1959).

Donoghue, Denis (ed.), *Jonathan Swift: A Critical Anthology* (Harmondsworth, 1971).

Foster, Milton P. (ed.), *A Casebook on Gulliver among the Houyhnhnms* (New York, 1961).

Gravil, Richard (ed.), *Swift: Gulliver's Travels* (Casebook series) (1974, repr. 1982).

Jeffares, A. Norman (ed.), *Fair Liberty Was All His Cry* (London, 1967)

Paulson, Ronald (ed.), *Satire: Modern Essays in Criticism* (Englewood Cliffs, NJ, 1971).

Probyn, C. T. (ed.), *The Art of Jonathan Swift* (London, 1978).

Rawson, Claude (ed.), *The Character of Swift's Satire: A Revised Focus* (Newark, 1983).

——, Claude (ed.), *English Satire and the Satiric Tradition* (Oxford, 1984).

Tuveson, Ernest (ed.), *Swift: A Collection of Critical Essays* (Twentieth Century views series). (Englewood Cliffs, NJ, 1964).

Vickers, Brian (ed.), *The World of Jonathan Swift* (Oxford, 1968).

Williams, Kathleen (ed.), *Swift: The Critical Heritage* (London, 1970).

Introduction

Clark, P., 'A Gulliver Dictionary', *Studies in Philology* L (1953), pp. 592–624.

Clifford, James L., 'Gulliver's Fourth Voyage: "Hard" and "Soft" Schools of Interpretation', in *Quick Springs of Sense: Studies in the Eighteenth Century*, ed. Larry S. Champion (Athens, Georgia, 1974).

Morrissey, L. J., *Gulliver's Progress* (Hampden, Conn., 1978).

Reiss, Timothy J., *The Discourse of Modernism* (London, 1982).

Said, Edward W., *The World, the Text, and the Critic* (London, 1984)

Walton, J. K., 'The Unity of the *Travels*', *Hermathena* CIV (1967), pp.5–50.

Watkins, W. B. C., *Perilous Balance: The Tragic Genius of Swift, Johnson, Sterne* (Princeton, 1939).

Wood, Nigel, *Swift* (Brighton, 1986).

Author-centred Approaches

Brown, Norman O., 'The Excremental Vision' (Tuveson, 1964).

Collins, John Churton, *Jonathan Swift: A Biographical and Critical Study* (London, 1893).

Craik, Henry, *The Life of Jonathan Swift* (2nd edn, London, 1894).

Dobrée, Bonamy, *English Literature in the Early Eighteenth Century* (Oxford, 1959).

Downie, J.A., *Jonathan Swift: Political Writer* (London, 1984).

Ehrenpreis, Irvin, *Swift: The Man, his Works and the Age* (3 vols, London, 1962–83).

Greenacre, Phillis, *Swift and Carroll: A Psychoanalytic Study of Two Lives* (New York, 1955).

Huxley, Aldous, *Do What You Will: Essays* (London, 1929).

Johnson, Samuel, 'Swift' in *Lives of the English Poets* (2 vols, O.U.P. London, 1906, repr. 1952).

Leavis, F.R., 'The Irony of Swift' (1934) in *The Common Pursuit* (1952 repr.1962).

Murry, John Middleton, *Jonathan Swift: A Critical Biography* (London, 1954).

Nokes, David, *Jonathan Swift, A Hypocrite Reversed: A Critical Biography* (London, 1985).

Orwell, George, 'Politics *vs.* Literature: An Examination of *Gulliver's Travels*' (1946) in *The Collected Essays, Journalism and Letters*, vol. 4 (Harmondsworth, 1970).

Sontag, Susan (ed.), *Barthes: Selected Writings* (London 1982, repr. 1983).

Stephen, Leslie, *Swift* (London, 1882).

Yeats, W. B. 'The Words upon the Window-pane' (play and preface) in *The Variorum Edition of the Plays of Yeats*, ed. Russell K. Alspach (New York, 1966, repr. 1979).

Formal and rhetorical approaches

Allen, Walter, *The English Novel* (1954, Harmondsworth, 1958).

Davies, Hugh Sykes, 'Irony and the English Tongue' (Vickers, 1968).

Davis, Herbert, 'Swift's Use of Irony' (Vickers, 1968).

Donoghue, Denis, *Jonathan Swift: A Critical Introduction* (Cambridge, 1969 repr. 1971).

Dyson, A. E., 'Swift: The Metamorphosis of Irony' (1958) in *Casebook*.

Ehrenpreis, Irvin, 'Personae' in *Restoration and Eighteenth-Century Literature*, ed. Carroll Camden (Chicago, 1963).

———, 'Swift and the Comedy of Evil' (Vickers, 1968).

Elliott, Robert C., 'Gulliver as Literary Artist', *ELH: A Journal of English Literary History*, XIX (1952), pp.49–62.

———, *The Power of Satire: Magic, Ritual, Art* (Princeton, NJ, 1960, repr. 1966).

———, *The Literary Persona* (Chicago, 1982).

Ewald, William Bragg, *The Masks of Jonathan Swift* (Oxford, 1954).

Frye, Northrop, *The Anatomy of Criticism* (Princeton, 1957).

Jefferson, D. W., 'An Approach to Swift' in *Pelican Guide to English Literature*, vol.4 (Harmondsworth, 1957).

Jordan, J. E. (ed.), *De Quincey as Critic* (London, 1973).

Karl, Frederick R., *A Reader's Guide to the Eighteenth Century English Novel* (New York, 1974).

Kernan, Alvin, *The Cankered Muse: Satire of the English Renaissance* (New Haven, 1959) (extract in Paulson, 1971).

Kettle, Arnold, *An Introduction to the English Novel* (2nd edn, 1954).

Knight, G. Wilson, 'Swift' (originally 'Swift and the Symbolism of Irony', 1939) in *Poets of Action* (London, 1967).

Leyburn, Ellen Douglass, *Satiric Allegory: A Mirror of Man* (Yale, 1956, repr. 1978).

Mack, Maynard, 'The Muse of Satire' (1951) (Paulson, 1971).

Paulson, Ronald, *The Fictions of Satire* (Baltimore, 1967) (extract in Paulson, 1971).

Price, Martin, *Swift's Rhetorical Art: A Study in Structure and Meaning* (Yale 1953, repr. 1962).

Quintana, Ricardo, 'Situational Satire' (1947) (Tuveson, 1964).

Rawson, C. J., *Gulliver and the Gentle Reader* (London, 1973).

Read, Herbert, *English Prose Style* (London, 1928).

Saintsbury, George, *The Peace of the Augustans* (London, 1916).

Steele, Peter, *Jonathan Swift: Preacher and Jester* (Oxford, 1978).

Williams, Ioan, *Sir Walter Scott on Novelists and Fiction* (London, 1968).

Historical and contextual approaches

Carnochan, W. B., *Lemuel Gulliver's Mirror for Man* (Berkeley, 1968).

Case, A. E., *Four Essays on Gulliver's Travels* (Gloucester, Mass., 1958, repr. of Princeton 1945).

Crane, R. S., 'The Houyhnhnms, the Yahoos and the History of Ideas' (1959) (Donoghue, 1971).

Downie, J. A., 'Political Characterization in Gulliver's Travels', *Yearbook of English Studies* 7 (1977).

Eddy, William A., *Gulliver's Travels: A Critical Study* (Princeton, 1923, repr. Gloucester, Mass., 1963).

Ehrenpreis, Irvin, *The Personality of Jonathan Swift* (1958, repr. New York 1969).

——, 'The Meaning of Gulliver's Last Voyage', *Review of English Literature*, III, 3 (July 1962).

Fabricant, Carole, *Swift's Landscape* (Baltimore, 1982).

Firth, Sir Charles, 'The Political Significance of Gulliver's Travels', extract in *Casebook*.

Frantz, R. W., 'Swift's Yahoos and the Voyagers', *Modern Philology*, XXIX (1931), pp.49–57.

Frye, Roland Mushat, 'Swift's Yahoos and the Christian Symbols of Sin', *Journal of the History of Ideas*, XV (1954), pp.201–17 (Foster, 1961).

Fussell, Paul, *The Rhetorical World of Augustan Humanism* (London, 1965).

Goldgar, Bertrand, *Walpole and the Wits* (Lincoln, Nebraska, 1976).

Higgins, Ian, 'Swift and Sparta: The Nostalgia of Gulliver's Travels', *Modern Language Review*, 78(3) (July 1983).

Kallich, Martin, *The Other End of the Egg: Religious Satire in Gulliver's Travels* (Brideport, Conn., 1970).

Kenner, Hugh, *The Counterfeiters: An Historical Comedy* (Bloomington, 1968) (extract in Donoghue, 1971).

Lock, F. P., *The Politics of Gulliver's Travels* (Oxford, 1980).

Louis, Frances D., *Swift's Anatomy of Misunderstanding: A Study of Swift's Epistemological Imagination* (London, 1981).

Nicolson, Marjorie, *Science and Imagination* (Ithaca, NY, 1962). (Contains 'The Scientific Background of Swift's Voyage to Laputa' (1935), with Nora Mola; and 'The Microscope and English Imagination'.)

Probyn, Clive T., 'Swift and Linguistics: The Context behind Lagado and around the Fourth Voyage', *Neophilologus*, 58 (1974), pp.425–39.

——, Clive T., *Jonathan Swift: The Contemporary Background* (Manchester, 1978).

Rogers, Pat, *Eighteenth Century Encounters* (Brighton, 1985). (Contains 'Gulliver and the Engineers'.)

——, 'Gulliver's Glasses' (Probyn, 1978).

Ross, Angus, 'The Social Circumstances of Several Remote Nations of the World' (Vickers, 1968).

Ross, John F., 'The Final Comedy of Lemuel Gulliver' (1941) in *Casebook*.

Stephen, Leslie, *History of English Thought in the Eighteenth Century* (3rd edn, 1902, repr. 2 vols, London, 1962).

Taylor, Aline Mackenzie, 'Sights and Monsters and Gulliver's Voyage to Brobdingnag', *Tulane Studies in English* (1957), pp.29–82.

Williams, Kathleen, *Jonathan Swift and the Age of Compromise* (Lawrence, Kansas, 1958, repr. 1968).

Wedel, T. O., 'On the Philosophical Background of Gulliver's Travels' (1926), repr. in *Casebook*.

Yeomans, W.E., 'The Houyhnhnm as Menippean Horse' (1966), repr. in *Casebook*.
Zimmerman, Everett, *Swift's Narrative Satires: Author and Authority* (Ithaca, 1983).

Appraisal

Anderson, W. S., 'Paradise Gained by Horace, Lost by Gulliver' (Rawson, 1984).
Lacasce, Steward, 'The Fall of Gulliver's Master', *Essays in Criticism*, XX (1970), pp.327–33.
Lucretius: *On the Nature of the Universe*, trans. Ronald Latham (Penguin Classics, Harmondsworth, 1951).
Reilly, Patrick, *Jonathan Swift: The Brave Desponder* (Manchester, 1982).
Ross, Angus, *Swift: Gulliver's Travels* (Studies in English Literature, London, 1968).
Selden, Raman, *A Reader's Guide to Contemporary Literary Theory* (London, 1985).
Traugott, John, 'The Yahoo in the Doll's House' (Rawson, 1984).

Further Reading

Paul Turner's edition of *Gulliver's Travels* (Oxford University Press, 1971) deserves mention for its valuable annotations. *The Correspondence of Jonathan Swift*, ed. Harold Williams (5 vols, Oxford, 1963–5) is an important and delightful resource for the researcher. Those who wish to relate the *Travels* to Swift's other writings will find *Jonathan Swift* edited by Angus Ross and David Woolley (Oxford, 1984) an excellent one-volume selection. Pat Rogers's edition of *The Complete Poems* is fully annotated and contains a useful biographical dictionary of Swift's contemporaries.

Index

Adams, R.M., 24
Allen, Walter, 28
Anderson, William S., 64

Blair, Hugh, 42
Bonner, W.H., 52
Bredvold, Louis I., 41, 44, 57
Brown, Norman O., 25–6

Carnochan, W.B., 15, 32, 52
Case, A.E., 31, 55–6
Clark, P., 13
Clifford, James L., 15
Collins, Churton, 63
Craik, Henry, 54
Crane, R.S., 43, 44, 48–9

Davies, Hugh Sykes, 40
Davis, Herbert, 40
Delaney, Patrick, 22
De Quincey, Thomas, 34
Derrida, Jacques, 16
Dobrée, Bonamy, 24
Donoghue, Dennis, 29, 32
Downie, J.A., 27, 56–8, 63
Dyson, A.E., 40

Eddy, William A., 14, 42–3
Ehrenpreis, Irvin, 36–7, 47–8, 49–50
Eliot, T.S., 14, 18, 33
Elliott, R.C., 30, 32–3, 36, 62
Ewald, W.B., 35

Fabricant, Carole, 60
Firth, Sir Charles, 54–6, 59, 60
Foucault, Michel, 16
Frantz, R.W., 43, 46, 52
Freud, Sigmund, 72
Frye, Northrop, 31
Frye, Roland, M., 46
Fussell, Paul, 44–5, 57

Gay, John, 20–1
Goldgar, Bertrand, 54

Gosse, Edmund, 14
Gove, P.B., 31
Greenacre, Phyllis, 25

Hawkesworth, John, 22
Hazlitt, William, 23, 64
Higgins, Ian, 50, 77
Huxley, Aldous, 19, 25

Jefferson, D.W., 39–40
Johnson, Samuel, 18, 20, 41, 67

Kallich, Martin, 49
Karl, Frederick R., 29
Kenner, Hugh, 53, 73
Kernan, Alvin, 27–8, 31
Kettle, Arnold, 28
Knight, G. Wilson, 39

Lacasce, Steward, 81
Landa, Louis, 48
Leavis, F.R., 17, 18–19, 38, 40, 47
Letter from a Clergyman to his
  Friend (1726), 21
Leyburn, Ellen Douglass, 32
Lock, F.P., 56–8
Louis, Frances D., 15, 53
Lovejoy, A.O., 44

Mack, Maynard, 34, 35
Miller, J. Hillis, 63
Monk, Samuel Holt, 15
More, John B., 34
Morrissey. L.J., 13
Murry, John Middleton, 25–6

Nicolson, Marjorie, 43, 44, 51–2

Orrery, Lord, 22
Orwell, George, 17, 24, 47, 62–3

Paulson, Ronald, 29
Pound, Ezra, 33
Price, Martin, 39
Probyn, C.T., 51, 52

Quintana, Ricardo, 34

Rawson, Claude J., 14, 26, 37, 40
Read, Herbert, 38
Reilly, Patrick, 62
Reiss, Timothy J., 16
Richardson, Samuel, 21, 22
Rogers, Pat, 59–60
Ross, Angus, 58, 67
Ross, John F., 47

Said, Edward, 16, 17
Saintsbury, George, 34
Scott, Sir Walter, 34, 54
Selden, Raman, 65
Sherburn, George, 48
Sheridan, Thomas, 23
Sontag, Susan, 18
Speck, W.A., 56
Starkman, Miriam K., 53
Steele, Peter, 32
Stephen, Leslie, 24, 25, 43–5
Swift, Deane, 22

Taylor, Aline M., 58–9
Thackeray, William Makepeace, 14, 23, 24
Tomashevsky, Boris, 65
Traugott, John, 68

van Doren, Carl, 33

Walton, J.K., 15
Watkins, W.B.C., 14
Wedel, T.O., 45–6, 48
Wesley, John, 22
Williams, Kathleen, 21, 47, 62–3, 77
Wood, Nigel, 16–17

Yeats, W.B., 19–20, 66
Yeomans, W.E., 47
Young, Edward, 22

Zimmerman, Everett, 15, 53, 69, 89